797,885 Books

are available to read at

www.ForgottenBooks.com

Forgotten Books' App
Available for mobile, tablet & eReader

ISBN 978-1-332-40853-5
PIBN 10423173

This book is a reproduction of an important historical work. Forgotten Books uses state-of-the-art technology to digitally reconstruct the work, preserving the original format whilst repairing imperfections present in the aged copy. In rare cases, an imperfection in the original, such as a blemish or missing page, may be replicated in our edition. We do, however, repair the vast majority of imperfections successfully; any imperfections that remain are intentionally left to preserve the state of such historical works.

Forgotten Books is a registered trademark of FB &c Ltd.
Copyright © 2017 FB &c Ltd.
FB &c Ltd, Dalton House, 60 Windsor Avenue, London, SW19 2RR.
Company number 08720141. Registered in England and Wales.

For support please visit www.forgottenbooks.com

1 MONTH OF FREE READING

at
www.ForgottenBooks.com

By purchasing this book you are eligible for one month membership to ForgottenBooks.com, giving you unlimited access to our entire collection of over 700,000 titles via our web site and mobile apps.

To claim your free month visit:
www.forgottenbooks.com/free423173

* Offer is valid for 45 days from date of purchase. Terms and conditions apply.

English
Français
Deutsche
Italiano
Español
Português

www.forgottenbooks.com

Mythology Photography **Fiction** Fishing Christianity **Art** Cooking Essays Buddhism Freemasonry Medicine **Biology** Music **Ancient Egypt** Evolution Carpentry Physics Dance Geology **Mathematics** Fitness Shakespeare **Folklore** Yoga Marketing **Confidence** Immortality Biographies Poetry **Psychology** Witchcraft Electronics Chemistry History **Law** Accounting **Philosophy** Anthropology Alchemy Drama Quantum Mechanics Atheism Sexual Health **Ancient History** **Entrepreneurship** Languages Sport Paleontology Needlework Islam **Metaphysics** Investment Archaeology Parenting Statistics Criminology **Motivational**

FALA AND SOUTRA

INCLUDING

A HISTORY OF THE ANCIENT

"DOMUS DE SOLTRE"

WITH ITS MASTERS AND GREAT REVENUES

AND OF OTHER HISTORICAL ASSOCIATIONS AND BUILDINGS

BY

JAMES HUNTER, F.S.A.Scot.
Minister of the Parish

WITH ILLUSTRATIONS

EDINBURGH:
JAMES G. HITT, 37 GEORGE STREET
PRINTED BY TURNBULL AND SPEARS
1892

Br 9881.2

HARVARD COLLEGE
MAY 4 1915
LIBRARY
Treat fund

PREFACE.

A FEW years ago, after giving a lecture on Soutra Monastery, a thought possessed me that an interesting history of the ancient " Domus De Soltre," and of the Parish generally, might be put into permanent form. The authorities that are given were consulted, and after several years of casual research, which has been a labour of pleasure and love, the present volume is the result. I have tried my best, without fear or favour, to give a faithful representation of men and things of the past; and now it is sent out with the earnest hope that the Parishioners, the Antiquary, and the general Reader will not only find it worthy of a perusal at the present, but also a book of reference in the future.

A list of Authorities has been given instead of the usual reference notes which often appear in similar works at the foot of the page; and the local spelling has also been retained, as " Isle " for " Aisle," " Beatsman " for " Beadsman," &c.

For much courtesy shown while consulting books, &c., best thanks are due to the Librarians of the Advocates'

Library, the Signet Library, and the Edinburgh University Library; to Mr Skinner and Mr Adam, of the Edinburgh Town Council Chambers; to the heads of several departments of the Register House; and especially to Dr Dickson, of the Historical Department.

For several of the Illustrations I am indebted to Mr Baird, agent for the Clydesdale Bank, Portobello; to Mr Ainslie of Costerton, and Mr Horn of Woodcote Park, for the loan of Photographs; and to Major-General Anderson, Edinburgh, who kindly gave the use of the Jacobite Relics in his possession, belonging to the Anderson family. The Illustrations were all reproduced by Photo-Zincography by Alexander Brown, Picardy Place, Edinburgh.

J. H.

Christmas, 1891.

ILLUSTRATIONS.

	PAGE
Exterior View of Soutra Isle,	*Frontispiece*
Fala Luggie, ...	*facing* 16
Silver Whistle of Prince Charlie, ...	„ 20
Gold Scarf-Pin with Prince Charlie's Hair, . . .	21
Portrait of Prince Charlie, ...	24
Woodcote Park, ...	40
Woodcote Park (East Front), ...	56
Mr John A. Ainslie, ...	60
Lord Wood's Coat of Arms, ...	63
Gilston Tower, ...	68
Fala Kirk, ...	72
Silver Communion Cup, ...	75
Kirk Token—Obverse and Reverse, ...	76
Fala Kirk and Manse, ...	80
Fala Manse, ...	88
The Rev. James Hunter, F.S.A.Scot., ...	, 96
Fala "Meetin' House,"	„ 128
The Seal of the Andersons of Whitburgh (showing enlarged impression),	„ 130
The Blair Seal (showing enlarged impression), . . .	„ 131

LIST OF AUTHORITIES
CONSULTED FOR THIS WORK.

Acts of General Assembly, Church of Scotland.
Ancient Taxatio, 1176.
Arnot's History of Edinburgh.
Archbishop's Tax Roll, 1547.
Bagimont's Roll, in vetera monumenta, by Theiner.
Bannatyne Club Publications—
    Book of the Universal Kirke of Scotland.
    Diurnal of Remarkable Occurrents till the Year 1575.
    Origines Parochiales Scotiae.
    Ragman's Roll.
    Registrum domus de Soltre, &c.
Bower's History of Edinburgh University.
Campbell's (Lord) Lives of the Chancellors.
Carlyle's (Dr) Autobiography.
Chalmers' Caledonia.
Chambers' History of the Rebellion, 1745.
Chambers' Lives of Eminent Scotsmen.
Clephane v. Town Council of Edinburgh, July 1874.
Dalyell's Fragments.
Dalkeith Presbytery Records.
Edinburgh Town Council Records.
Edinburgh University Commissioners' Report, 1837.
Edinburgh Town Council v. Edinburgh University, 1824.
Exchequer Rolls of Scotland.
Fala Kirk-Session Records.
Forbes on Tithes.
Forsyth's Beauties of Scotland.
Fordun's Scotichronicon.

List of Authorities.

Gordon's (Dr) Monasticon, &c.
Hailes' (Lord) Catalogue.
Hamilton Papers, The (1890).
Hay's (Father) MSS.
Hayne's State Papers.
Hogg's Jacobite Relics.
Index to Great Seal Charters, MSS. Signet Library.
Jamieson's Dictionary.
Maitland Club Publications—
    History of the Kirke of Scotland.
    Registers of Ministers, &c.
Maitland's History of Edinburgh.
Maps—
    Armstrong's Three Lothians, 1773.
    Forrest's Maps of East Lothian, 1779.
    Pont's and Adair's MSS. Maps, 1608.
Nisbet's Heraldry.
Privy Council Records of Scotland.
Prynne's History.
Registers of Great Seal Charters.
Retours, Service of Writs, &c.
Rodgers' (Dr) Social Life.
Rymer's Faedra.
Spottiswoode's Religious Houses.
Scott's (Dr) Fasti Scotiae.
Turnbull's Fragments.
Woodrow's Church History.
&c.   &c.   &c.

CONTENTS.

CHAPTER I.

INTRODUCTION.

PAGE

Derivations of the words "Fala," "Soutra"—Situation—View from Soutra—Streams—Linndean—Roads, ... 1

CHAPTER II.

FALA KIRK AND PROPRIETORS.

Fala Kirk—Rectory—Proprietors—Hays—Edmonstones—Sinclair—Hamiltons—M'Gill—Stair, ... 6

CHAPTER III.

DIVISIONS OF FALA PARISH.

Fala Parish—Divisions of Property—Brothershiels—Fala Moor—King James V.—Fala Flow—Salvandi—Fala Luggie—Cakemuir Castle—"Frostineb"—Blackshiels—Inn—Fala Dam—Prince Charlie—Fala Mill—Fala Hall, ... 14

CHAPTER IV.

VILLAGE OF FALA.

Fala Village—James V.—James VI.—Sir John Cope—Lord Chancellor Eldon—Decline—Smith, ... 23

Contents.

CHAPTER V.
MONASTERY OF SOUTRA.

Soutra—Girthgate—Watling Street—Monastery—Early Charters—Gifts of Lands—Wealth of Monastery—Importance—Confirmation by Pope Gregory IX.—Hospicé—Trinity Well—Sanctuary—Soutra Isle—Order of St Augustine—Special Protection—Names of Masters—Soutra Monastery Mill—Prior's Well, ... 30

CHAPTER VI.
TRANSFER OF SOUTRA REVENUE.

Soutra Monastery or Holy Trinity Hospital—Transfer of Revenues—Of Name—Erection of Trinity College Hospital, Edinburgh—Prebendaries—Soutra Vicarage Church—Vicars—Beadsmen—Pringle, . 45

CHAPTER VII.
LANDS OF SOUTRA.

Soutra Lands—Soutra Beacons—The Hertford Invasion—"Surety Men"—Hunter's Hall—Lawrie's Den—Soutra Witch—Mr John Ainslie—The Deil's Putting Stone, ... 53

CHAPTER VIII.
PROPRIETORS OF SOUTRA.

The Geology—William Borthwick—Robert Fletcher—Pringles—Maitlands—Reidhall—Falconers—Sir Thomas Napier—Mrs Ogilvie—Woodcote—Lord Wood—Lord Justice-General Inglis—Mr Lothian—Mr Crombie—Mr Horn—Gilston Tower—Proprietors of Gilston—North Brotherstones and Proprietors—Andersons of Whitburgh—Kellybaak and Johnstounburn Proprietors—Keith Marischal, . . . 62

CHAPTER IX.
CHURCH OF FALA.

Fala Church—Furnishings—Communion Cups—Bell—Churchyard—Mort Cloth—Fala Manse—Glebe—Patronage—Right of Presentation—Sale of Right of Presentation, ... 72

Contents.

CHAPTER X.
MINISTERS OF THE PARISH.

Thomas Cairns, the last Roman Catholic Vicar—The Rev. Messrs Frank, Johnstoun, Henderson, Hastie, Carkettill, Carmichael, Thomsone, Porteous, Logan, Moodie, Johnstoune, Grant, Cavers, and Simpson—Battle of Prestonpans—The Rev. Messrs Wotherspoon, Gourlay, Sprott, Singers, Sherriff, Harkness, Munro, Ingram, Thomson, and Hunter, ... 83

CHAPTER XI.
STIPEND OF FALA.

Stipend—Return to Ecclesiastical Commissioners in 1627—Down Grade—Uncertain Value—Unexhausted Teinds, ... 100

CHAPTER XII.
RECORDS OF KIRK-SESSION.

Kirk-Session Records—Volumes I., II., III, IV., V.—Quaint Extracts—Register of Baptisms—Register of Proclamations—Register of Burials, 110

CHAPTER XIII.
BOARDS OF THE PARISH.

Parochial Board—School Board—Schoolmasters—Libraries—Charities—Friendly Society, ... 117

CHAPTER XIV.
FALA SECESSION CHURCH.

The Secession Church—Its Origin—Ministers—Sir William Johnston—Congregation—Anniversary, ... 123

CHAPTER XV.
EMINENT MEN CONNECTED WITH THE PARISH.

Eminent Men—Andersons of Whitburgh—John Logan—Rev. William Anderson—Farm Tenants—Agriculture—Wages—General Condition of the People, ... 129

Contents.

CHAPTER XVI.

CHARACTER OF PARISH AND PEOPLE.

The Perfect Rural Character of the Parish—The General Condition of the People—What they Read—Their Intelligence—Their Religion—Their Inquisitiveness—Their Politeness—Conscription—Home Life—Change in Food—Their Work—The Land Question—A Solution—A Blessing, ... 141

GENERAL INDEX 151

Fala and Soutra.

CHAPTER I.

INTRODUCTION.

Derivation of the words " Fala," " Soutra "—Situation—View from Soutra—Streams—Linndean—Roads.

THE name "Fala" is derived from the little hill upon which the Parish Church stands, and is a contraction for Faulaw, Fawlaw, or Falla. It is the same Fal or Faw which is found in Falkirk, Falkland, and Fauside, and means "speckled," hence Fala means "speckled hill." In some of the old charters it is designated "lie Falla,"—"lie," a corruption of the French article "le," showing that the French influence was considerable at Court and in Law. The use of the article was meant to mark it off from the smaller Falas that then existed in various parts of the country.

Soutra, spelt Soltre, Solter, Sowtray, Soutray, means, in the Cambo-British, "prospect town." No doubt the name arose from the magnificent view which is got from the site of the ancient monastery, which was at one time surrounded by a considerable village.

The question has been often asked, Where is Fala? and

Fala and Soutra.

the manner of asking indicated that the enquirer thought that Fala was either in the North Seas, the West Highland glens, or in the wilds of Connemara. Many will be surprised to learn that it forms the south-east corner of the county of Mid-Lothian, and is distant from the city of Edinburgh only fifteen miles. It is bounded on the east by the parish of Humbie; on the south by the parish of Soutra; on the west by Heriot and Stow; and on the north by the detached parts of Borthwick, Cranstoun, and Humbie, and by an attached part of Crichton parish. It is about five miles long from east to west, and one mile broad from north to south, and contains about 3120 imperial acres. Soutra, which is almost of the same length and breadth, lies immediately to the south, in the county of East Lothian, having Channelkirk for its southern boundary, and containing about 2940 acres. The great road, made in the year 1834, between Edinburgh and Lauder, is the line which marks off the cultivated lands to the east, from those which are mostly pasture to the west. The various white and green crops of the district are cultivated with success; and the parish has been long known to raise sheep which command the highest prices at fair and market. After entering the parish from the north, the ascent is gradual until you reach the summit of Soutra Hill, which is about 1230 feet above the level of the sea.

At this point a wide expanse of country opens to your view. Mr Singers, in Sinclair's "Statistical Account of 1794," says:—" The view from Soutra is most enchanting. Passing for a considerable way through the dreary moor, where nothing meets the eye but barren heath, here, all at once, the fine cultivated counties of Mid and East Lothians, with the Frith of Forth and coast of Fife, burst upon the view. The suddenness of the change, and the mingled group of hills, and dales, and woods, and waters, which now stretch extensive to the eye, give such a throb of pleasure to the heart as is not to be described." Even in the clear atmosphere of April and September there may be seen far beyond the Pentland range the cone-shaped tops of Ben Lawers and Ben Ledi; and farther to the east, on a clear, sharp winter's day, after a fall of snow, there is reflected the general outline of the Sidlaw Hills in Forfarshire. The Isle of May, with its bright electric flash at night; the Bass Rock, North Berwick, and Traprain Law, all come within the visual range. But seldom will the spectator find within such a short radius so many beautifully-situated mansions. Elphinstone Tower, Oxenfoord Castle, Prestonhall, Ormiston Hall, Saltoun Hall, Humbie House, Costerton House, Whitburgh, Woodcote Park, and Johnstounburn, may be all seen from Soutra Hill. The Firth of Forth, from Dunbar to the Bass Rock, and from Fidra Lighthouse to Cramond Island, is distinctly seen; even the Castle Rock of Edinburgh, struggling hard to rise above the smoke, is conspicuous.

The centre of the united parishes may be considered the watershed between the tributaries of the Gala on the west, and the Tyne on the east. Cakemuir Burn, rising in the moss about the famous castle of that name, runs north-east, under the high embankment of the Lauder road towards Fala dam, and joins the Linndean Burn beyond the mansion of Keith. Fala Hall Burn rises in the moor to the south of Fala Flow, and forms the boundary between Fala and Soutra parishes, —leaves Deanburn, the residence of Mrs Dods, through the lands of Woodraik and Fala Hall, and joins the Cakemuir Burn above Costerton. The Linndean, by far one of the prettiest streams in the Lothians, starts in the Hens Moss to the west of Lawrie's Den,—rushes on to a wild and deep and rocky gorge, and forms a splendid cascade clothed by birch and oak and mountain ash, and falls into Kate's Cauldron, a deep pool named after a Miss Cathrine Maitland, daughter of the Laird of Soutra, who drowned herself two hundred years ago, in a state of frenzy over a love affair. After leaving the pool, it gurgles on between high rocks on either side, over boulder and shingle for about 500 yards, until it comes to the open grounds around the mansion of Woodcote. It then passes on through Johnstounburn and Humbie Woods to join the Cakemuir Burn.

The Armet, which is the boundary between Channelkirk parish and Soutra, rises in the bog to the west of Lawrie's Den, and passes Gilston and Nether Brotherstone, and joins the Gala below Crookstone Castle. It receives at Nether Brotherstone the Brothershiels Burn, which is the boundary line between Fala and Soutra on the west.

The beautiful undulations of the soil—the uniform divisions of the lands caused by these streams—the natural situation on the northern slopes of the Lammermuir Hills, and the fir plantations on the moor and hills to the southwest, make the climate salubrious, although the air at times is bracing and sharp. Fogs are seldom seen, and the rainfall on the lower grounds is only 29 inches per annum. Often when the Lothians are covered with mist and fog in winter, the higher grounds are enjoying the bright and warm sunshine.

Parish Roads.

While the temperature rises sometimes to 70° F. in the shade in summer, the thermometer indicates during frosty nights 14° below zero in winter. The climate may yet be much improved by the draining of Fala Moor and Fala Flow, which are 1100 feet above the level of the sea, and also by a plantation on Soutra Hill. Although it is bleak and cold at times, the district is healthy, for the air is a blend from the mountain and the sea.

The parish, like the surrounding district, is well supplied with good roads. The two parishes, Fala and Soutra, are both bisected from east to west with an ancient road. The old moor road, which runs past Brothershiels, is simply a continuation of that which runs through Fala village from Johnstounburn and East Lothian. The other, coming from the east, passes Soutra Mains, the Isle—the ruins of the ancient monastery—Gilstoun, and Nether Brotherstones, and on to the Gala Road at Crookstoun Castle.

To the west of the present highway to Lauder can be traced what is called the King's Road, which, it is supposed, was made by Malcolm IV. to cross the Lammermuirs to Lauderdale. Girthgate or Sanctuary Road runs from the Isle to Cross Chainhill to the south, the privileged ground of the monastery; and Watling Street or Roman Road can be traced at various places on the hills towards Channelkirk.

CHAPTER II.

FALA KIRK AND PROPRIETORS.

Fala Kirk—Rectory—Proprietors—Hays—Edmonstones—Sinclair—
Hamiltons—M'Gill—Stair.

UP to the time when the two parishes were united in 1618, there seems to have been little or no connection between them. The rectors of Fala up to the Reformation, from the complete silence as to their names and functions, seem not to have been on friendly terms with their greater and richer neighbours on Soutrahill. In all the charters and historical references there is not the slightest notice of the priest who served the Fala altar, and supplied the spiritual wants of the Fala people. Yet there is a historical reference to the existence of a church at Fala prior to the oldest date in connection with the monastery of Soutra. In the ancient "taxatio of 1137" Fala Kirk had to pay, as its proportion, the sum of six merks, while there is no reference to Soutra, as the church and hospital there were the property of the Master and Brethren, and not subject to the same taxation. It is supposed that the Rectory of Fala was, like the other churches in Mid-Lothian during the tenth and eleventh centuries, under the diocese of St Cuthbert. The patronage of Fala, up to the present time from the eleventh century, has continued with the Lord of the Manor. It is supposed that there were associated with the Rector of Fala, some of the Brethren of the Trinity friars who had charge of a small hospital in connection with Fala Church; and this is supported by an entry in the Exchequer Rolls of Scotland, of date 1365, which states that the Brethren of the Holy Trinity of Fala had received from Robert de Erskyn, treasurer, the sum of £3, 6s. 8d.; and Forbes, in his Book on "Tithes," mentions that the order of the Trinity friars was appointed and confirmed by Pope Innocent III. (1200). Their *beneficies* were called *ministries*, and the prelate was called minister. Such were the ministers of Fala, Peebles, Scotland's Well, &c.

The Rectory of Fala, as it stood under James V., was taxed at £6, 13s. 4d.; and it again appears in the Archbishop's Tax Roll of 1547.

Of the teinds as well as of the minister nothing can be said; but in all likelihood, as the church was under the immediate patronage and supervision of the Lord Superior, the minister would be paid by him according to some rule approved of by the Bishop. The church and rectory would be upheld from the same source, under the spiritual supervision of the Bishop of St Andrews, who held sway over the Lothian churches up to the Reformation. The proprietors of the lands of Fala were better recognised by the Master and Brethren on Soutrahill than were the Rectors of Fala. In the early Soutra charters there appear the names of Sir **Bartholemow de Fawlay**, Samuel de Fawlay, and Adam de Fawlay, these gentlemen taking the names of their estates, as was common at the times. Father Hay mentions that the name of Sir Edward Hay, first laird of Fawlay and Linplum, appears in a charter of his brother David, granting him the lands of Fala. This Sir Edward was a second brother of the House of Yester, and the charter is dated, "Apud castrum de Peebles, 10th August

1439." In 1429, Agnes de Fawlay was paid the sum of £14 by William Nory, Treasurer, Edinburgh, for seventeen ells of cloth which she supplied to the Royal Household. Agnes may have been the wife of the laird. John Hay, who was killed at the battle of Verneull in France, was father to Sir William Hay of Fala, as appears by a charter of David, Lord Yester, to Sir William of Fala, dated August 1469. The Hays, it may be presumed, were the Lords of the Manor up to the time that the lands fell into the hands of the Edmonstouns of that Ilk. Early in the beginning of the sixteenth century the Edmonstouns were the chief proprietors of the lands in the parishes of Newton, Liberton, Cranstoun, Crichton, and Fala, as well as of Ednam in Roxburghshire. The first charter relating to the Edmonstouns in the Great Seal charters of Scotland, is that of date the 15th May 1533, which says that the King (James V.) confirmed the charter by James Edmonstoune on the one part, and Adam Hume and Janet Edmonstoune on the other part, of their lawful and just right to the lands of Edmonstoun, Ednam, &c., with the gift of the Churches and Chapels, and to the right of the patronage of the hospital of Fala.

The lands of Fala were destined soon to pass from the Edmonstouns, and, whether by marriage or otherwise, the Sinclairs of Roslin became proprietors. In 1542, the King (James V.), at Edinburgh, confirmed the charter of the lands of Fala to Sir William Sinclair of the Roslin Militia. Sir William could play not only at *land-grab*, but also at *button-grab*, for, in the Privy Council Records, it is recorded that at Holyrood House on the 6th July 1573 appeared "Sir William Sinclair of Rosling, Knycht, who was charged to give, exhibit,

The King's Buttons.

and produce before my Lord Regent's Grace, and Lords of Secret Council certane buttonis of gold sumtyme pertenan to owre Soverane Lord's Moder, given to him in pledge, contanand in number sextene dosane, and deny the ressait thairof, affirmed that Mr Thomas Makcalyeane had ressavit the same, whereupon the said Mr Thomas, being called to answer *super inquirendis*, confessed the ressit of sa mony buttonnis of the wecht foresaid fra the said Sir William Sinclair, by virtue of his writing, under his subscription containing the selling and deliverance thairof made by him to the said Maister Thomas for the sowme of fyve hundreth merkis ressavit to him for the samyn, wherefore the said Maister Thomas, being charged to make exhibition, exhibit the same of the number and wecht foirsaid desyrit ane day to call the said Sir William for his warrand." The buttons were afterwards returned to the Lord Regent, and Mr Thomas was allowed to take action against Sir William, which was settled out of court. The Sinclairs were not long in possession, for in 1597, the King confirmed a charter made by John Hislop, Master of the Hospital of St Leonard's in Edenhame, by which David Edmonstoun of Charterhouse was to be given back the lands in fee simple of Spittal-Kellaflat, also the lands of Fala, Fala Hall, Brothershiels, and Woodraik (Longwood), with the hill and mill lands and the teinds. This charter was witnessed by Francis Edmonstoun at his residence, Fala Hall House, on the 11th October 1596.

The last of the Edmonstouns who was proprietor was named Patrick. His name appears in the deposition which was made by the parish minister and others, before the Presbytery of Dalkeith in 1627, when a Royal Commission, which was appointed to enquire as to the Ecclesiastical Revenues of the Church, appeared. The next name that appears in connection with the lands of Fala is that of David Creichton of Lugtoune-Creichton, who was served heir to the lands and teinds on the 22nd November 1649. It cannot be ascertained whether this property came into the Creichtons by purchase, by theft, or by gift. Though they were not long in possession, the family kept up a connection with the parish for many years afterwards. The Laird's son became schoolmaster at a salary from the Kirk-Session of £40 a year. He also acted as reader in the Church. The grandson was educated at Edinburgh University from the Session Funds, and afterwards succeeded his father as parochial teacher, acting in that capacity up to the Revolution settlement. Shortly before his resignation, a scandal arose in the parish which created a great amount of feeling, and which caused his resignation. In the newly-erected mansion of Fala, called Fala House, which stood about half-a-mile south-east from the Parish Church, lived a Lady Humby, whose two servants, Patrick Craig and Jane Hanson, were summoned before the Kirk-Session for scandalous conduct. They refused to appear, as it afterwards turned out, by the private advice of David Creichton, who was also summoned for his connivance. After a long and protracted consideration of the case by the Kirk-Session, the three were all, in the face of the congregation, rebuked by the minister, which gave so much offence to Lady Humby that she left the parish, and gave as a solatium to the poor the sum of five pounds.

In 1662, Patrick Hamilton of Little Prestoun, son and heir of Mr Patrick Hamilton, was served heir to the lands of

Fala, &c., with the teinds in augmentation of £20, 13s. a-year. This marks a very important epoch in the history of the parish, as the lands up to the present time had remained in the same family connection, and as he was the first to erect a family residence, lay out the grounds, and plant with firs and other trees a large portion of the estate. Patrick, as far as can be learned from the Register, had three children—Thomas, who became proprietor in 1674; Jean, who became, in 1699, the wife of William Blackwood, merchant, Edinburgh; and John Hepburn Hamilton, who was named after the Laird of Humbie, and who became a Colonel, and was witness to the baptism of three of his brother's children.

Colonel Thomas Hamilton succeeded his father Patrick, and had a large family, four of whom were baptised in Fala Kirk. Thomas, son of the Colonel, was served heir in 1742. He had been married for several years before he came to own the lands, and he, like those who had gone before, took up his residence in Fala House. There were two children of the marriage—Thomas, who was born in October 1736, and Elizabeth, born in November 1737. At Elizabeth's baptism in Fala Kirk there were as sponsors, " My Lord Oxford and Sir John Dalrmple." The first, no doubt, was meant for Baron Oxenfoord, and the second was son of the Sir John Dalrymple, who, by his connection with the Massacre of Glencoe, left an indelible mark on Scottish history. Their presence at this baptism is significant, for this little lady was destined to bring together by marriage the three great houses that were represented, viz., the houses of Hamilton, Dalrymple, and M'Gill. Tradition throws a humorous light upon Elizabeth's marriage. It is said that Sir John rode from Cranstoun and met his lady-love unknown to both parents at the Fala House Lodge, which was situated on what is now the Joiner's Park, thirty yards west from the south corner of the Glebe. They were careful to have witnesses present, who could prove if necessary that she ran away with him, and not he with her. Before they mounted the same horse she was heard to exclaim, "Come on, John!" A start was made, and soon she was

> "O'er the border and awa'
> Wi' Jock o' Fordel-dean."

Thomas, the brother of Elizabeth, when he came to heir the Fala estates, took the name Thomas Hamilton-M'Gill; and afterwards, when the estates came to her, she was known as Lady Dalrymple Hamilton M'Gill, wife of Sir John Dalrymple, Bart., of Cousland.

After the annexation of the various properties, the proprietors of Fala ceased to live in Fala House, and although it was occupied by tenants up to the beginning of the present century, it was allowed to fall into decay. That which was once one of the finest country mansions, and the scene of domestic felicity, is now no more. The old armour which made it famous was removed to Oxenfoord Castle, and the stones of the building itself were carted away to build that which has been known for the last eighty years as Blackshiels Inn. Although the mansion was neglected, much has been done to improve the value of the land by plantation on the east of the moor, and by drainage and other means. As much of the land to the west of the parish is only of prairie value, an extension of the present woods would not only give better shelter to stock, but would further improve the climate, and might yield a better return for timber than what is presently got as rent from tenants. The old spirit of Hamilton of Fala, who set the good example to the neighbouring proprietors of enclosing his estates by hedge and ditch, and by sheltering his fields with clumps of trees, is worthy of being revived, and thereby giving, not only beauty to the landscape, equality of temperature to the atmosphere, but also greater shelter to man and to beast.

The Stair family are still in possession of the lands of the parish, which are all let to tenants.

CHAPTER III.

DIVISIONS OF FALA PARISH.

Fala Parish—Divisions of Property—Brothershiels—Fala Moor—King James V.—Fala Flow—Salvandi—Fala Luggie—Cakemuir Castle—" Frostineb "—Blackshiels—Inn—Fala Dam—Prince Charlie—Fala Mill—Fala Hall.

THE following divisions of the parish of Fala, which is entirely owned by Lord Stair, are recognised in the old charters, and also in the old locality of stipends—Fala, Fala Hall, Brothershiels, and Woodraik, or Longwood. Brothershiels forms the western part of the parish, and lies up against Nettlingflat and Hangingshaw, in the parish of Heriot; both were for long in the possession of Soutra Monastery. On the Nettlingflat road there existed for long a common piece of pasture of about twenty-five acres, which was used by gipsies and drovers for feeding and resting cattle, but several years ago a march fence was run through it, giving the one half to Brothershiels and the other to Nettlingflat. To the east of Brothershiels, stretching for about three miles, and one mile broad, lies the well-known Fala Moor. It has been made historical by King James V. in 1542 resting there for a few days an army of thirty thousand men. King Henry of England, under the pretext that he was Lord Superior over Scotland, that James had broken faith in not keeping an appointment to meet and arrange State affairs, and also that James had been found guilty of connivance with the Irish rebels, declared war against Scotland. A great muster took place on the Boroughmuir, Edinburgh, and after all necessary arrangements were made, the king and his army marched southwards through Dalkeith, Pathhead, and the village of Fala, to the muir. After bivouacking there for a few days, news arrived of the marching of the English army. The king held a council with his nobles, and it was agreed upon that Earl Huntly should proceed with a thousand men, and those behind should prepare to give battle. After Huntly had left, and as the English were not so near as was anticipated, discontent broke out among the nobles, whom the king again summoned to his presence, and tried to pacify by appealing to their devotion and patriotism. He made a long speech, of which the following is a part:—" Shall it ever be said that the nobility of Scotland have abandoned the services of their king in the sight of the enemy, and when the two armies were ready to engage? Is it possible that you, who have courted opportunity to shew your bravery, would willingly lose this opportunity which offers when you may purchase fresh laurels?" The leaders could not agree, and the army was disbanded.

The king, shortly after he had left Fala, got intimation that a daughter had been born to him, when he exclaimed, "It came with a lass, and will go with a lass." The religious feeling of the country, the news of the defeat of the army at the Solway, where so many were taken prisoners, the discontent of the nobles, and the birth of a daughter, all preyed upon his mind, and filled him with rage, shame, and regret. His health soon gave way, and he died a few weeks after his visit to Fala Moor at Falkland, in the flower of his age.

In the middle of Fala Moor is situated Fala Flow, a

small loch about a quarter of a mile long. It is believed by some of the inhabitants that the loch has no bottom, as its water is of a dark, peaty colour. There are many stories of horses and men having been drowned in crossing the moor, by coming in winter upon the morass which surrounds the Flow. Of all the stories, the following appeals most to the imagination :—A gentleman on horseback was crossing the moor on one occasion, when horse and rider suddenly disappeared. They were never seen in this country again; but it appears that three weeks afterwards they were found, safe and sound, in New Zealand, having fallen straight through the earth to the other side.

The Flow is a natural resort of wild ducks and geese, and other fowls. There is only a solitary house occupied by the shepherd, upon the moor, called Salvandi, the name taking us back to the time when "the church on the hill" was supreme. The name is the Latinised form, and may mean the place of salvation or safety.

On the north side of the moor a scar may be seen, where for generations the villagers and minister got their peats for fuel; but the development of the coal-fields at Arniston and Newbattle has put all in the district beyond the need of a peat fire.

Near to the scar is situated the remains of an old Roman speculum or keep, called Fala Luggie. Of its history nothing is known; but as it is situated on that part of Watling Street which runs from Soutra to Currie, near Borthwick Castle, it is either the ruins or the site of a Roman look-out. There can be no doubt that the Romans lived there, for two Roman urns were found in 1852, a few hundred yards

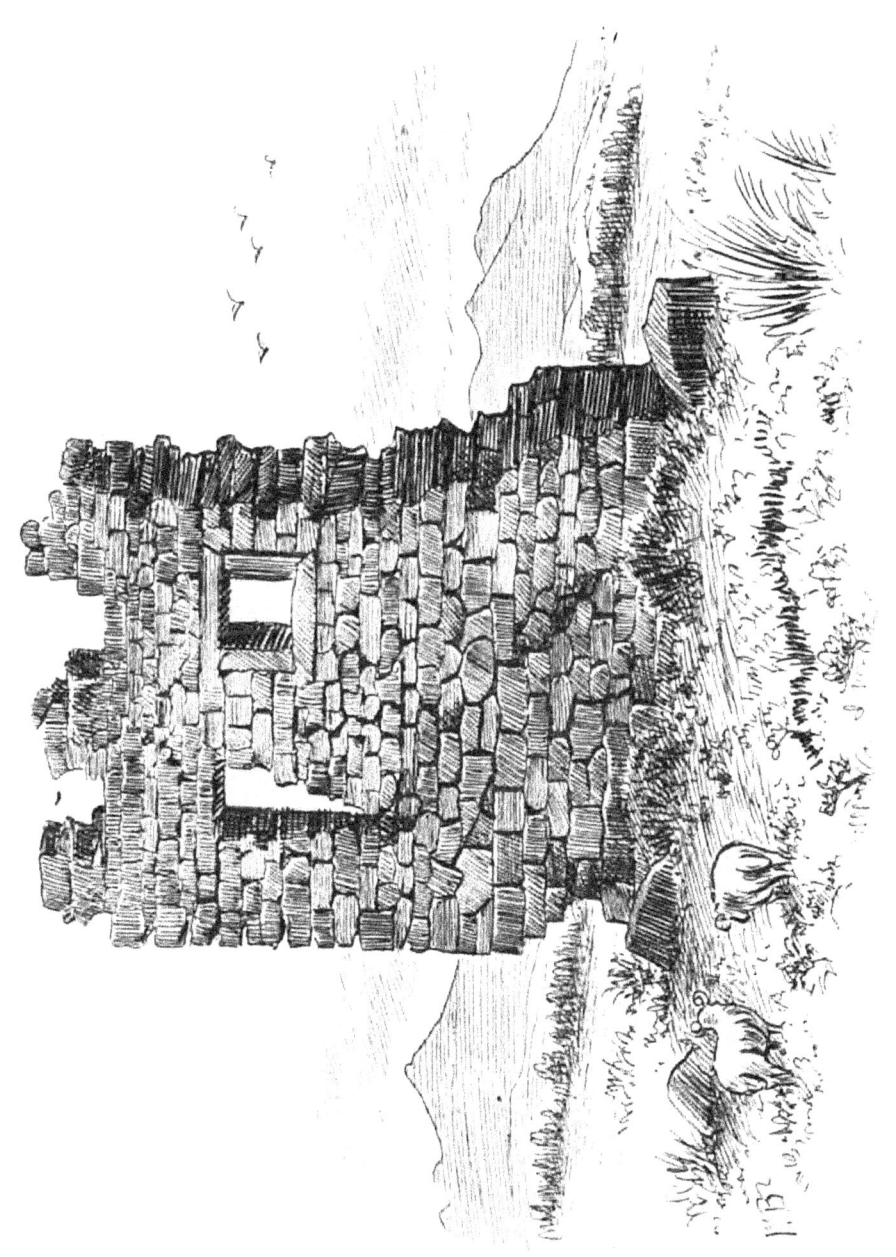

FALA LUGGIE.

to the north, on Cakemuir Hill. They were presented to the Museum of the Society of Antiquaries, Edinburgh, by Mr Borthwick of Crookstone. Several coins were found at the ruin about the same time, belonging to the reign of Charles I. The ruin itself is now not much, and shows that utilitarian hands have been upon it again and again. It commands a magnificent view of the Pentlands, Arthur Seat, and Mid-Lothian, and a most likely place to erect a signalling station. Around it are still to be found faint traces of a ditch or moat, and beyond the land has been cultivated. Overlooked by the Luggie is the ancient castle of Cakemuir, where Queen Mary slept the night after she fled from Borthwick Castle. She went from Cakemuir to Carberry Tower, where she met the Earl Bothwell.

The castle itself was only a square, strong tower, in much decay, until it fell into the hands of the present proprietor, Mr George Wight of Edinburgh. It has been thoroughly repaired; stained glass windows put into the room where the Queen slept; and also a large wing has been built in harmony with the older building. The whole building is now in first-class condition, and reflects the greatest credit upon the present laird, who occupies it during the summer months. The lands around, like others in the district, are held in feu, and were once in possession of the House of Soutra. About the time of the Reformation they were acquired by the Wauchops of Niddrie, who were in possession for over three hundred years, when they were sold to Alexander Mackay, the son of a successful border drover. Mackay held them until 1880, when they were purchased by the father of the present laird. To the east, and still overlooked by the Luggie, is West Mains, which is better known as " Frostineb," a name which the property does not in any way suggest. It also has been purchased by Mr Wight. Adjoining this property to the east is the well-known Blackshiels, the shieling of the Blackfriars, from whom it originally got its name. The monks possessed it for long. Little is known of the other proprietors until the land was held by the Kers, late of Woodburne, Dalkeith, who owned it for over a hundred years. It was sold to Lord Stair forty or fifty years ago.

The great increase of vehicular traffic between Edinburgh and the south brought into existence, about the beginning of this century, the well-known Blackshiels Inn. It grew step by step, until now it is, for size, a formidable building on the east side of the new public road of 1834. A great trade was carried on, not only in supplying the wants of the neighbouring people and sportsmen, but also of numerous travellers who came by coach. When the railways were opened in 1842, there were thirteen coaches, which passed each way every day. There were twenty pairs of horses, and vehicles of all kinds, constantly kept at the inn. It was a stirring place. Farmers from Lauderdale, from east and west, met to transact business and to drink deep. It was no uncommon thing for farmers who had been at the Thursday Dalkeith market never to think about going home until their wives, who came to church on Sunday, came to the rescue. Their Sunday's worship was a fitting penance for three days' debauch. All this is now changed. The inn is now occupied by Mr Broomfield, son of the last keeper of the inn, as a dwelling-house. He farms the lands of Blackshiels, Fala Mill, and Fala Parks. The post office and another dwelling-house are all that now remain of a once flourishing village. Although situated near the village of Fala, Blackshiels is a detached part of Humbie Parish, in the county of East Lothian; and the Boundary Commissioners, appointed under the County Council Act of 1890, have declared that it should be in Fala Parish, County of Mid-Lothian. Soutra is also put into Mid-Lothian. When the Commissioners had this matter under their consideration, an attempt was made by Mr Ainslie of Costerton, and Mr Slimon of Whitburgh, and others, that Costerton and Haughhead of Costerton should also be declared to be in Fala Parish; but the Crichton Parochial Board, who were asked to approve of the transfer, decided by a majority against it. The Commissioners on that ground refused. It was known to them that this matter of parochial boundaries is an old grievance, for, in 1627, when Commissioners were appointed under Charles I. to examine into the ecclesiastical affairs of Scotland, the minister and parishioners of Fala petitioned that Costerton, Fala Dam Feus, and Cakemuir should be in Fala Parish. The petition was refused on the ground that the Commissioners had no powers.

Fala Dam takes its name from the mill dam or lade which was situated a little above the ford over the Cakemuir Burn. That half of the village which is situated on the north of the stream is in Crichton Parish, and the half on the south side is in Fala. The old Edinburgh road passed through this village for ages, and the bridge which now crosses the stream was erected about the middle of last century. The mill has now been abolished for fifty years, and the village, like other parts of the parish, is decreasing in population year by year. It was here where Prince Charlie and his suite were entertained by the

Andersons of Whitburgh after the Battle of Prestonpans in 1745. When the Prince and his army were encamped above Tranent Muir the night before the battle, they were considering the best means of attacking the army of Sir John Cope, when one of the Generals informed the Prince of a young man who knew the ground, and was willing to lead the army by the best and safest path. This young man was the son of the Laird of Whitburgh. He knew the ground well, for, being a keen sportsman, he often shot over it, as part of it belonged to an uncle. Young Anderson was admitted into the presence of the Prince, who received him favourably, as he had learned of his knowledge of the place, and as the Andersons were well known to be strong Jacobites. He accomplished the task, which led to a disastrous result to the Whig army. The Prince never forgot this act, and, when passing Fala for the south, made a halt at the Dam to receive the Anderson family. On the 31st October 1745, the Prince, with an army of six thousand, left Musselburgh for Dalkeith, where they halted for the night. The army here divided into two portions. One, under the command of Lord George Murray, took the road to Carlisle by Peebles. The other left Dalkeith on the 3rd November, with the Prince marching at their head, and arrived at Prestonhall Gate, where he had breakfast, which was prepared by the

Silver Whistle of "Prince Charlie," in possession of Major-General Anderson, C.B.

Prince Charlie Relics. 21

orders of the Duchess of Gordon, who occupied Prestonhall at that time. After leaving Prestonhall, the next halt was Fala Dam, where the Prince and his suite had luncheon, which was prepared and served by the young ladies of Whitburgh House. After a little attention on his part, and when he was about to leave, the ladies asked for a keepsake. Immediately he cut from the hilt of his sword a piece of embroidered red cloth (not a piece of velvet, as is sometimes narrated), and handed it to them. The Prince and army marched on through Fala Village, over Soutrahill, and had refreshments again at Lawrie's Den, and finished the first day's march at Lauder town. Major-General Anderson, C.B., of Drumsheugh Gardens, Edinburgh, the last of the Andersons who possessed Whitburgh, has in his possession the relic of the Prince, and several other historical articles which the Prince had gifted to the family at various times. The following articles are in General Anderson's possession. A miniature enamelled portrait of the Prince sent by him after he had left the country to Robert Anderson of Whitburgh, as a remembrance of his services at the Battle of Prestonpans, 1745. A gold scarf pin with small lock of the Prince's hair. Two small silver seals. Two sleeve buttons worn by the Prince at his balls at Holyrood after the battle in 1745; and a silver whistle which he used before the same battle. These invaluable relics of a chivalrous Prince might be procured by the nation for national

Gold Scarf Pin, with Prince Charlie's hair, presented to the Andersons of Whitburgh.

purposes; although the Andersons guard them with feelings of pride.

About the beginning of this century, Fala Dam was in a high state of excitement by the discovery of the body of a lady in one of the old houses. It appears that a Lady Forrester had made her escape, or had decamped from her residence about Corstorphine. She made her way southwards, and when she reached Fala Dam, exhausted by cold and fatigue, she crept into an old dilapidated house to die, where her body was found next day by her relatives.

Adjoining the lands of Fala Mill, and opposite Costerton, lies Fala Hall, one of the best farms in the parish. It takes its name, "Fala Hall," from the fact that, before Fala House was built by the Hamiltons, and upon it stood the residence of the early proprietors. The Hays of Fala would reside here. The house itself is old and quaint, inhabited by the tenant, and the farm now also includes that of Fala North Mains. Several relics of a bygone age have been found. Two cists or stone coffins were got when draining the field to the west of the steading fifty years ago, and in 1865 a celt of sandstone, $10\frac{1}{2}$ inches by $3\frac{1}{2}$ inches, was also discovered, and was presented to the Museum of the Society of Antiquaries, Edinburgh, by Mrs John Scott. Various articles of bronze at different times have been found, but these now cannot be traced. All this is a great proof that Fala Hall must have been inhabited, and the lands cultivated, at an early period of Scottish history.

CHAPTER IV.

VILLAGE OF FALA.

Fala Village—James V.—James VI.—Sir John Cope—Lord Chancellor Eldin—Decline—Smith.

THE village of Fala is the most important centre in the parish, having the Church and manse, the school and school-house, the U.P. Church and manse, and all those necessary concomitants that go to make up a village. It is often confounded with Blackshiels, as it lies against it, the division not being visible to the stranger. It is entirely in the parish of Fala, Mid-Lothian, was at one time situated on the main road from Edinburgh to Lauder, and became a place of considerable importance. It is only since the great road was opened in 1834, which passes within a hundred yards of the village, that it has become obscure, and eclipsed by its neighbour Blackshiels, through which the new road passes. In fact, Blackshiels only came into notice after the first quarter of this century by its inn and post office.

In the olden time the village of Fala was a convenient resting-place for travellers, amongst whom may have been kings and queens, nobles and squires, knights and common people. King James V., when passing with his army in October 1542 to Fala Moor, stopped at the village and signed a confirmation charter, granting to William Menteith de Kerse, the lands and barony of Kerse, &c., &c. On the 6th September 1547, five years after, the Queen (Mary), at

Fala, granted by charter to George, Earl of Rothes, the lands and barony of Ballinbriych, and also another charter, granting the lands of Leslie and Kennoway. But as the Queen was only five years of age, a minor, and resident at the time in Stirling, she could not have in person granted these two charters. As Earl Huntly had been on the West Marches at the time, and had been appointed Governor of Scotland a few months before, and had got word that the English army was marching northwards by Berwick, he, in passing Fala four days before the disastrous battle at Pinkie, Musselburgh, in all likelihood, in name of the Queen, granted these charters.

The village of Fala was honoured by another Royal visit of some importance on Friday, the 12th October 1593. King James VI. made a proclamation at Edinburgh on the 9th October 1593 for a great muster at Lauder. It may be as well to notice that there were two great parties in the State at the time, who were each plotting and planning for their own interest and for the management of affairs. There was the Bothwell party, the chief of whom were the Earls of Athole, Montrose, and Gowrie. There was also the party of the forfeited and fugitive Catholic lords, led by the Earls of Huntly, Angus, and Errol. The King hated the party that the clergy favoured, that of the Bothwell party. Shortly before, the Synod of Fife, which met at St Andrews, proclaimed the Earls of Huntly, Angus, and Errol, Lord Hume, Sir Patrick Gordon of Auchindoun, and Sir James Chisholm, excommunicated, idolaters, heretics, &c., &c. This was proclaimed in every presbytery and in every parish in Scotland, feeling against them was so strong. The King also issued a proclamation

PORTRAIT OF "PRINCE CHARLIE."

(In possession of Major-General Anderson, C.B., Edinburgh.)

condemning the Catholic earls, under the belief that they were engaged in the Spanish plot. Agreeably to the proclamation of the 9th, the King and his suite left Edinburgh on the 12th, and halted at Fala village at the close of their first day's march. The Catholic lords, Huntly, Angus, and Errol, learning of the departure of the King, and as they knew that an interview with him would be more likely to be successful out of Edinburgh, where feeling against them was running strong, followed in the route to Fala. When the King had halted, they advanced into his presence, and, throwing themselves at his feet, entreated his pardon. The King was greatly perplexed, as he knew that these lords were excommunicated by the Church, and that feeling was strong against them, dreaded lest it should be thought that the meeting had been pre-arranged. The King summoned such councillors as were with him, and with their advice made an arrangement with the suppliant Catholic earls to the effect that they should stand a trial, and clear themselves if possible.

With that view they were also to enter themselves in ward at Perth on the 24th October, and there to abide until tried. The earls left Fala rejoicing, and the King went on his way to Jedburgh.

News soon arrived in Edinburgh of this strange meeting at Fala, which caused great excitement. A great meeting of the clergy was called to discuss the matter, who condemned the temporary arrangement with the excommunicated lords. A deputation was appointed, and sent to the King with a petition to Jedburgh. He, when he received the petition, flew into a rage, dismissed the deputation, and promised to see the matter arranged for himself. The excusant lords took advantage of the lull in their troubles, and fled to France, and their estates were soon afterwards confiscated by the Crown.

After the battle of Prestonpans, in 1745, the routed army of Sir John Cope flew from the disaster to the Lammermuirs, passing Fala. The village people received into their homes some of the soldiers, and hospitably entertained them, moved by a kindred feeling, as their minister and several men from the farms around had been engaged in the battle. Up to recent years soldiers were often billeted in the village, which caused the people to hold the soldier in terms of the highest respect.

Another event of some historical importance, although of a different character, took place in the village in November 1772—viz., the marriage of Lord Chancellor Eldon.

Lord Eldon, whose family name was John Scott, was the son of a Newcastle miner, who opened a small shop in Love Lane of that town, and as it proved of moderate success, he was enabled to educate his children at the best schools. John was born on the 4th June, 1751, went at an early age to school, and left for the University of Oxford in 1766, where he intended to complete his studies for the Church. During his holiday he courted Elizabeth Surtees, the daughter of a well-to-do Newcastle banker, very much against the wish of her parents. On the night of the 18th November 1772, an elopement was made by placing a ladder against the window of the first floor of Mr Surtees' house, and down it came the young lady, assisted by one Wilkinson, who had also a post-chaise waiting a short distance off. The young pair drove off unknown to any of the relatives, and made their way by

Morpeth and Coldstream to Soutrahill and Fala. When they arrived at the village they asked the parish minister, Mr John Gourlay, to marry them, but he refused, as they had not complied with the laws of the Church. A post boy from the inn was immediately dispatched for the nearest Episcopal minister, who was at Haddington. The minister in time appeared, and John Scott, Student at Oxford, and Elizabeth Surtees, were duly married in that house which is presently used by the Fala baker. In this connection often Fala and Blackshiels are confounded. In Blackshiels proper, there was only at that time a small public-house, the inn being on the opposite side of the road, and newly built. The following certificate of marriage was preserved by him up to his death:—

> "John Scott of the Parish of All Saints, Newcastle-upon-Tyne, gentleman, and Elizabeth Surtees of St Nicholas Parish, in the same town, were married at Blackshiels, North Britain, according to the form of matrimony prescribed and used by the Church of England, on this the nineteenth day of November, 1772, by James Buchanan, Minister.
>
> In presence of } JAMES FAIRBAIRN, Witness.
> THOMAS FAIRBAIRN, Witness."

The two witnesses were father and son, and occupied Fala Inn, Blackshiels, at the time. The newly married couple hurried off after the marriage, and never halted until they arrived at Morpeth, where arrangements were made for their accommodation by Mrs Walsh of the "Queen's Head," who had given up her own room for the occasion. The marriage alienated the sympathy of both their parents, which caused John Scott to give up the idea of studying for the Church. However, his elder brother, unlike the one in the parable, came to his rescue, and materially assisted him in prosecuting his studies. By his marked ability and faithful labours he rose to fill one of the most honoured positions in the land; and after years of devotion to duty, died Lord High Chancellor of all England.

Few villages have had such a rapid decline as that of Fala. It is not now the fourth of the size it was sixty years ago. It had its doctor, policeman, inn, several public houses, shops of various kinds, tailors, joiners, and blacksmiths in abundance. Now these have mostly all disappeared, and the closing of the Blackshiels Inn ten years ago, and the stopping of the coach, have left it without stir or bustle. Houses after houses have disappeared, and are disappearing, some of which at the present time are in a very dilapidated condition, and unfit for human residence. The famous blacksmiths of Fala have now only one representative. During the coaching days the smithy was a place of some importance, there meeting all and sundry, discussing the kirk and market, the laird, the minister. The blacksmiths were usually hired from year to year, as the hinds are hired at the present time. Often the under-smith went under the name of hind, a name common still in the district. About the beginning of this century the Fala smith was named John, and was as usual quite a character. He became the subject of the well-known nursery rhyme, the author of which is unknown. It is as follows :—

> "John Smith, Fala hind,
> Can ye shae a horse of mine?

The Fala Smith.

Yes, indeed, and that I can,
Just as well as any man ;
I'll put a bit upon the tae,
To make the pony tak' the brae ;
I'll put a bit upon the heel,
To make the pony trot weel !
Trot weel !! trot weel !!!"

CHAPTER V.

MONASTERY OF SOUTRA.

Soutra—Girthgate—Watling Street—Monastery—Early Charters—Gifts of Lands—Wealth of Monastery—Importance—Confirmation by Pope Gregory IX.—Hospice—Trinity Well—Sanctuary—Soutra Isle—Order of St Augustine—Special Protection—Names of Masters—Soutra Monastery Mill—Prior's Well.

THE most outstanding historical feature connected with the parish is the Hospital of the Holy Trinity, which stood on the summit of Soutrahill, overlooking the Lothians to the north.

Before the existence of Girthgate, which passed through the King's Inch, a small piece of ground lying to the south, which for long was the resort of gipsies and tramps, the only access to the Hospital was by the Roman Watling Street. Watling Street crossed the borders at Carter Fell, through the parish of Oxnam, and straight towards Lauderdale, through which it passed to Channelkirk and Soutrahill. From the hospital it formed one straight line to Currie, in the parish of Borthwick, passing Fala, Luggie, Cakemuir, and Blackcastle.

There can be no doubt but the hospital, in whatever shape it first existed, found its existence on the side of Watling Street. It is possible that the Romans had there, as at Channelkirk, a camp or fort, which grew after years into a retreat for the traveller and the devout. It may have existed long before the first historical notice. The common opinion that it was founded by King Malcolm IV., in the year 1164, rests only upon the authority of the "Continuator of the Scotichronicon, who wrote about the middle of the fifteenth century." He says, "In the year 1164, by the consent of Walter Abbot of Melrose, King Malcolm founded the nobile monasterium de Cupro in Angus, *et ante hoc coenobium de Soltrey ad viatores hospitandos.*" This only shows that before the year 1164 the monastery was founded. As he does not give the source of his information, it may be supposed that he got it from the king's charter, which contains the grant of the lands of Brotherstanes extending to the Linndean, the greater part of Soutra parish. But this charter, granted between 1153 and 1165, the period of the king's reign, has no date, and makes no reference to the Hospital as being newly founded. Of its great wealth and influence there can be no doubt. Chalmers, in his "Caledonia," says that it was "the best endowed in Scotland," and the existence of the original chartulary, containing fifty-eight charters, on twenty-seven leaves of vellum, in the possession of the Faculty of Advocates, gives proof to this.

The following is an account of the enormous wealth which this ancient Hospital enjoyed for many years, as given by the charters that are extant. The gifts are arranged, as far as can be, chronologically.

(1) King Malcolm IV. granted the lands of Brotherstanes, up to and including the lands of Lyndean. This grant was renewed with extended privileges by his brother, William the Lion, and again confirmed by Alexander III. Lands, *men*, &c., were included.

(2.) David Oliver grants 12 *sheaves* of corn yearly, and all his tenants are to give one sheaf from every cart-load in harvest. It is supposed that his lands lay near Melrose.

(3.) Philip of Ew gives the lands of Philipstoun, Ew, with one toft and croft, and the two acres of land next to it which Peter, son of Albert, held of the Holy Trinity Hospital, along with common pasture for 2 horses and 7 oxen.

(4.) Richard, son of Michael, of Peaston, grants 4 bolls of corn, *clean* and *good*, yearly from the lands of Peaston. He afterwards gifted his whole lands, with all the common pasture in the village of Peaston, to upkeep one chaplain in the House of Soutra, to serve perpetually for the living and the dead.

(5.) John, son of Robert Russell of Duncanlaw, gives half oxgang of land, with the toft and croft of half an oxgang from his lands. The master and brothers also set land at Duncanlaw, "*for male yheirly* for 10s. and 3 *caponis*."

(6.) Eustacee of Stuttenel grants 2 measures of oatmeal from his lands in Ledale, yearly, at the feast of the passover (Easter.)

(7.) Flora, (widow) of the late Ade Quintin, bequeaths all the arable land at Lympetlaw, which is named Welflat, with the toft and croft adjoining that land.

(8.) Bernard of Hauden gives annually at the feast of St Nicholas 4 bolls of corn.

(9.) Peter de Graham grants 3 oxgang of land, the toft and croft, and right of common pasture on his farm, in the Barony of Elphinstoun.

(10.) Vinean Mulineys gives half a ploughgate of the lands of Saltoun for *pure* and *perpetual* charity. The whole lands were shortly afterwards, by the same person, gifted, and were measured off by Sir Walter Olifard, Justiciary of Lothian, by command of the king's lord.

The monastery also possessed in Saltoune, Leys land, which gave 7s. yearly.

(11.) The Abbot and Convent of Dryburgh grant all the tithes which the same brothers ought to pay to the mother Church of Channelkirk, from the ploughgate of land belonging to them in the parish of Channelkirk, which is called Futhewethynis, towards Wedale (Stow), in return for one pound of *pepper* and one pound of *cymin*, at the fair of St James, Roxburgh.

(12.) John de Methkil (ancestor of the Earl of Wemyss), by the motion of divine piety, gives the church of Wemyss, with all the privileges and pertenents, within and without. This grant was confirmed by David, Bishop of St Andrews, and afterwards by Gamelus, Bishop of St Andrews, 1262.

(13.) William Memil grants 1 acre and 3 poles in the town of Langtone ; and 2 acres and 4 poles near Millrig.

In Langtone the monastery also possessed a property let for 6s. 8d a year.

(14.) John de Stirling gives 2 acres from his lands of Ochiltree, with the right of common pasture for 4 cows and 12 sheep, with their progeny of one year, and also one thrave of corn from every ploughgate of his in autumn.

(15.) Thomas de Haye grants a thrave of corn from every single ploughgate of his lands on the south side of the sea, at harvest.

(16.) William, Bishop of St Andrews, gives the church lands of St Egidius (St Giles), Ormistoun, with all the teinds and other things rightly belonging to the said church. The monastery of Soutra presenting a clergyman to serve the church at Ormistoun.

(17.) Thomas de Restilrig gives one half chalder of corn, to be paid yearly.

(18.) William, Bishop of St Andrews, grants the church of St Martin's, Stratheycyn, Forfarshire, with all the lands and teinds and other things rightly pertaining to the same. Soutra in return presenting a clergyman to serve the church of St Martin's.

(19.) Charles de Duncan grants 34 acres of land and 2 acres of meadow on the estate of Swanston, to be held on the condition of an annual payment of a pair of spurs at Haddington fair. The H. T. of Soutra also get the right of common pasture for 24 cattle and their following, 2 horses, and 200 sheep.

He and his wife Mariot further grant 23 acres of land, along with the toft and croft held by Adam the Blacksmith; also common pasture for 60 sheep, 10 private horses, and 2 work horses.

They further grant 10½ acres of land, along with the right of common pasture for 2 work horses, 10 private horses, and 60 sheep.

Alexander II., in 1225, confirms by charter the gifts of the lands of Swaynstoun.

(20.) Thomas de Craynstoune confers the right to cultivate that portion of Cranstoun which lies next to the lands of Peaston.

Radulph, Lord of Craynstoun, grants the lands of Cranston, which (from the description of the boundaries given) are Sauchland, Blackcastle, and Tynehead.

William de Craynstoune, notary, granted a charter in 1399

of all the lands of Craynstoune possessed by the house of Soltre, and instructed Thomas de Aldtoun, at that time master, to make a perfect inventory. The monastery also possessed a property which gave yearly 6s. 8d.

(21.) Richard Germyne gifts the church of Lympetlaw, with all the lands and teinds and other things belonging to the same.

He also grants the other lands of Lympetlaw held by him.

(22.) Walter, Bishop of Glasgow, confirms the gift of the Church of Orde (Kirkurd), and all its pertenents which had been in the possession of the Monastery for some time, in 1231; again confirmed in 1255.

(23.) Nicholas of Old Bridge, and Annabella, his wife, convey the lands of Old Bridge and Swaynstoune to the House of Soltre.

(24.) Edward of Whitewell gives all his lands of Whitewell, his tenements in Swaynstoun, his lands in Mount Lothian and Temple. The House of Soltre to grant a priest to officiate three days a week at Whitewell.

(25.) Hugh, son of Augustine of Moravia, in 1249 granted 2s. to be paid annually by the tenant of the mill at Wyston. William also granted 4 bolls of oatmeal yearly.

(26.) John Marishall de Keith grants all the lands of Upper Johnstoun with the mill. This is now Woodcote Mains and Mavishall.

John of Johnstoun grants the lands of Lower Johnstoun by consent of Robert de Keith, Marescall of Scotland; but as the master and brothers felt the yearly feu-duty of 6 merks a burden, the charter was declared null and void by consent.

(27.) Walter of Soltre, Burgess of Berwick, granted his

lands and buildings, with free entrance and exit for all time coming. This was afterwards confirmed by another charter.

(28.) Alexander II., in 1229, granted half a chalder of oatmeal from the mill at Peebles to be paid yearly.

(29.) Thomas of Ercildoun, son and heir of Thomas Rymour of Ercildoun, in 1294 grants all his lands with all his belongings. The Monastery had also property in Earlston which gave 20s. yearly.

(30.) David de Grame of Elotistoun comes under the obligation to pay yearly half mark in silver as rent for 5 acres of land which the Monastery possessed at Whiterig

(31.) The Abbot of the Holy Cross of Edinburgh granted, in 1326, 6s. to be paid yearly.

(32.) The Master and Brothers of the House of Soutra held tenements in Lauder giving 9s. yearly; in Musselburgh, which yielded 300 dried fish and 3s. a year; in Haddington, which gave one pound of cumyn and 1s. 6d. yearly; in Whittynghame, 15s.; in Duns, 6s. 8d.; Heriot, 20s.; Maxtone, 10s.; Hawick, 6s. 8d.; Innerleithane, 2s. and 2 dozen of foullis; and North Berwick, 10s. a year.

(33.) In 1459 Sir William Lauder gave half an acre of his lands in Cowgate, Edinburgh, and Donald Gill gave a perpetual grant of 20s. yearly value. The Hospital also possessed the two pounds lands in the village of Falawhill, parish of Heriot, and the 5 merks lands in the parish of Newlands. The following yearly rents were also received:—2 merks from houses in Leith, 2s. from Allanson's and Lawson's houses in Leith, 20s. from the village of Risiltoune, 20s. from lands of Wauk in Edinburgh, 5s. from the house of Thomas, Bishop of Dunkeld; 6s. 8d. from village of Lauder, 6s. 8d. from

Privileges of Monastery.

Strathmiglo, and 10d. from Linlithgow. There was also a croft in St Leonard's, Edinburgh, which belonged to the Monastery.

(34.) In the Exchequer Rolls of Scotland there is notice of the following payments being made—William St Clair, Sheriff of Edinburgh, 4 bolls of corn (1290); Sir Robert of Peebles, 8 bolls for 2 years (1329), which was paid yearly for some time afterwards.

To manage so much property in these days was no easy task. In such an important house there must have been a large staff of qualified servants to perform the various duties that were incumbent upon them. The Master and Brethren would not only require to superintend those that were under them, but to be continually watchful of those who were ever ready to play at the game of grab, for grab was common even then. In 1271 Walter of Moravia refused to give to the Master and Brethren of the House of Soutra a thrave of corn from every ploughgate of his lands, which had been gifted by one of his ancestors. An appeal was made to Alexander III., who commanded an inquisition to be held at Roxburgh. Four persons were selected from each of the baronies of Upper Crailing, Eckford, and Heton, as judges in the matter; and they decided in favour of Soutra. On the approach of Edward I. to Scotland, Thomas, the Master of the Hospital of the Holy Trinity at Soutra, did homage and swore fealty to him at Berwick in 1296; and obtained in return orders to several sheriffs to deliver the estates and rights of the Hospital which had been appropriated by them. They were all secured.

The House of Soutra, as it was called, possessed many privileges as well as endowments. Not only were the

Brethren and their lands exempt from general taxation, and their persons protected by royal command, but also, according to the ancient charter of Malcolm the Maiden, the house was recognised as an hospital for the relief of pilgrims, a shelter for the support of the poor and afflicted, and a sanctuary to protect those who sought refuge from their troubles. All this was afterwards, by authority of Pope Gregory IX., confirmed by charter, which runs as follows:—

"Pope Gregory, servant of servants of God, to his beloved sons in the Lord. We have graciously granted your reasonable request; and we have taken the Church of the Holy Trinity of Soltre under our protection, and that of the Blessed Peter. We ordain that the religious order which has been instituted in that place, according to God, and the rule of St Augustine, shall be strictly preserved in all time coming; and whatever possessions you now have, or shall in future obtain by the bounty of Kings, Rulers, Chiefs, or others, shall be inalienably preserved; the place in which the Church is situated, with all its belongings, its aforesaid lands, pastures in mountain and plain, waters, mills, roads, paths, and all other things shall be retained by you; within the bounds of your parish no one shall erect a new chapel or oratory without your consent, and that of the Bishop of the Diocese. We also ordain that those who have stated in their last will and testament that they wish to be buried there, shall have the free right of burial; such teinds as belong by right to your Churches, but which have been appropriated by laymen, shall be delivered up by them to the Churches to which they rightly belong on the death of the present Master of the House of Soltre, or any of his successors. No one shall be appointed to the office except with the consent of a majority of the Brethren. If in future any person, ecclesiastic, or layman, aware of this writing of confirmation, shall do anything contrary to the tenor thereof, let him know that he thereby renders himself liable to Divine punishment, and becomes alienated from the Most Holy Body and Blood of our Redeemer, the Lord Jesus Christ; but upon all who keep these laws, may the peace of our Lord Jesus Christ descend, and may they have the reward of everlasting peace. Given at Rome by the hand of Mr William, Vice-Chancellor of the Holy Roman Church, on the 12th of the kalends of October, in the year 1236 A.D., and the tenth year of the Pontificate of Pope Gregory the 9th. Amen."

This charter is the first indication of the Monastery being under the protection and influence of the Roman Catholic Church.

Being situated half way between Holyrood and Melrose, in one of the healthiest parts of Scotland, and in such a commanding situation, it need not be wondered at that it became the scene of ostentatious charity and great conviviality during the middle ages. The religious pilgrim, the traveller, and the health-seeker would find in abundance that which they were in search of. There were the shrines and the altars to attract the devout; there were the free hospitality of a wealthy hospice to entertain the wayfarer; and there were not only the medical knowledge which the monks in those days possessed, and used for the good of the people, but there was also a mineral well, which became famous, and was frequented by thousands up to the Reformation.

To the north of the Monastery, about 400 yards, was

situated Trinity or Ternity Well, a spring of water clear and cool, which was a popular resort, and from which the Brethren would acquire some fame, as the waters were considered to be of a miraculous character. This well disappeared in the drainage of the field some years ago.

This place, having also the character of a sanctuary, would be largely frequented by those who fled from the wrath that was coming. They were not confined to the precincts of the building, for a chain surrounded the hill to the south to mark off the privileged ground which they might enjoy. Of the building itself now little remains to indicate its size or shape. The Isle, as it is called, is supposed to be a part of the ancient Church, restored by the Pringles in 1686, who were the proprietors of Soutra for about thirty years. It is simply a plain, square vault, arched with stone within, and covered with turf without, and used as a private burial-place.

In every likelihood the monastery would extend to the south and west of the present building. The present churchyard, which is contiguous to the building, may have been the cloister court. The stones and foundations have all disappeared; even the very stones that were erected to the memory of the Protestant dead have been taken away to build steadings and to repair dykes. Dr Laing, when he visited the place in 1860, spoke as if this vandalism had only taken place ten or twelve years before, and as if the Isle itself had only escaped from the same fate by the prompt exertion of the proprietor. Until recently a fine gargoyle graced the apex of the front, but it, too, has gone the same way. There is a monumental stone in the south end erected by the Pringles of the Beedsman's Acres to mark the spot of their burial, which

WOODCOTE PARK.

Order of St Augustine. 41

is supposed to be near. The lintels of the front entrance show traces of ancient sculpture work. There is also the following—" 16 D. P. A. R. 86." Some one has made the last P. into an R. It means David Pringle and Alexander Pringle, 1686.

There is no trace of the order, if they had any, to which the Master and Brethren belonged, until, by their own wish, the Pope placed them under the Order of that of St Augustine. It is generally supposed that St Augustine himself never founded any monastic order, but one was deduced from his writings, and was adopted by many monastic fraternities. The Soutra monks belonged to that branch called Canons Regular, or the Black Canons, from the black cloak or hood which they wore over their long cassock. Their rule was not severe. They lived under the one roof, having a common dining hall and sleeping room. There can be no doubt but the names of many of the places arose with them—Blackshiels, the sheiling of the Black Canons; Brothershiels, the sheiling of the Brothers; Brotherstanes, the stony ground of the Brothers. All these names are characteristic of the places and early owners. They elected their own Superior, who carried the title of Master, and who was usually a person of some importance, influence, and power. They travelled over Europe, and sometimes, like others, got into trouble. In consequence of the insecurity of the traveller, King Alexander I., in the year 1182, granted to the Master and Brethren of the House of Soltre, " that if they, or any of theirs, shall be in lands beyond the King's dominions, they shall be treated with right and justice wheresoever they shall be, and all in any country are prohibited from presuming to detaining them in any place."

From the Soutra charters, Spottiswoode's Religious Houses, Prynne's History, The Ragman's Roll, Chalmers' Caledonia, and Turnbull's Monastico-Fragmenta, a very interesting list of the Masters and others of the Hospital may be given. The list may not be complete, but every means have been used to make it as much so as possible.

(1.) About the end of the twelfth century, Sir Reginald, Master of the House of Soutra, is witness to several charters.

(2.) Sir William, in every likelihood Sir Reginald's successor, also gives his name to charters as witness.

(3.) In 1204, Alexander, Magister de Soltre, is a witness to grants by charter.

(4.) About 1290, Radulphus de Soutra is witness to a charter. He swore fealty to Edward I. of England at Edinburgh Castle, on the 29th July 1291.

(5.) In Ragman's Roll occurs—"Frere Thomas, ministrie de la meron de la Trinite de Soltre del counte de Edinburgh." On the 20th August 1296, he swore fealty to Edward I. at Berwick, and got Royal permission to instruct the sheriffs to return certain lands that had been stolen.

(6.) In 1390, Dominus Thomas de Alton, Master of Soutra, is witness to a charter. His name again appears in 1401 in a charter granted at Scone by Robert III., giving, by consent of the Bishop of St Andrews, the whole lands and rents and other things belonging to the Nunnery of S. Berwick, to the Monastery of Dryburgh. He was also master in 1410.

(7.) In one of the Soutra charters, dated the 4th March 1426, appears the name of Stephen Flemyn, Master of Soutra.

(8.) His successor is Thomas de Lawder, a distinguished

student and gifted divine. He is witness to charters in the years 1437-1439, and 1440. In 1444 he founded a chaplainry at the altar of SS. Martin and Thomas, in the Holy Cross Isle of St Giles, Edinburgh; and this endowment was confirmed by Royal charter in 1450, and was afterwards renewed and extended by himself, and confirmed by James III. in 1481. Lawder was promoted to the See of Dunkeld, as a reward for his services as preceptor to King James II. He was then sixty years of age, and was the first to adopt preaching in his diocese. Before he resigned his benefice, owing to old age and infirm health, in 1476, he saw the perversion of the House of Soutra to a different purpose, much to his regret.

(9.) In the year 1453, Alan Cant became Rector of the Hospital of Soutra, and Chancellor of the Church of St Andrews, which latter appointment he received from Pope Nicholas V., who annexed Soutra to the Church of St Andrews, by the influence of Bishop Lawder, and by consent of Cant himself.

He was a St Andrews student, and died there in 1460.

(10). In 1460, John Tyry became his successor. He was one of the masters elected assistant to the Rector of St Andrews.

Amongst the minor officials were—Master Hugh of Brotherstanes; Henry the Priest; William the Miller; Reginald and William, Chaplains, who both became Masters; Richard the Priest, and his servant; Edulph of Cakemore; Gilbert, son of the Priest of Heriot; Pradium Andrea of Soutra, Priest; Sir William and Adam, Chaplains at

Soutra; Hugo of Johnstoun; Sir Nicholas, Chaplain of Soutra; and Adam, the Janitor.

The mill under the auspices of the Soutra Hospital was situated about 1½ miles north-east from the Hospital, on the side of the Linndean burn. A road or footpath, which connected the two places, passed a little to the north of the present Woodcote mansion, and several parts of the road can still be traced. On the side of this path, and within half a mile of the mill may still be found the well called the "Friars'" or "Priors' Well," from which the monks of old, as we are told, as they passed, stopped to quench their thirst. It is a spring of beautiful clear and cool water, and is presently used by those who occupy Woodcote Park.

CHAPTER VI.

TRANSFER OF SOUTRA REVENUE.

Soutra Monastery or Holy Trinity Hospital—Transfer of Revenues—Of Name—Erection of Trinity College Hospital, Edinburgh—Prebendaries—Soutra Vicarage Church—Vicars—Beadsmen—Pringle.

THE Hospital of the Holy Trinity at Soutra was not destined to enjoy their possessions long, for in the year 1462, the widow queen of James II., Mary of Gueldres, with the consent of James Kennedy, Archbishop of St Andrews, founded the Trinity College and Hospital in Edinburgh, and bestowed upon it the endowments of Soutra Hospital, and converted its dependent church into a vicarage.

The first negotiations began in 1460, when the Queen was under deep affliction by the accidental death of her husband caused by the bursting of a cannon at Roxburgh Castle. The foundation of the Trinity Hospital at Edinburgh was simply a transfer of the revenues and name. The charter is dated 1st April 1462, and on the 10th July 1462, Pope Pius II. granted a bull reciting the Queen's charter, transfer, and foundation, a part of which, rendered into English, is as follows:—

"James, by the grace of God, and the Apostolic See, Bishop of St Andrews, to all the sons of the Holy Mother Church, to whose knowledge the present letters shall come, greeting; and felicity from the Saviour of all men.

"The splendour of the eternal glory which illuminates the world with its unspeakable brightness, and with all its great clemency, prosecutes with a special and benign favour the pious desires of the faithful when their humble devotion and sincere affection are found to be zealous for the increase of public worship. We therefore take example by things below from those above, are induced partly by the power of equity, and partly by reason to favour the godly requests and prayers of supplicants whom faith, hope, and charity incessantly solicit to show their love by benefactions, that being disposed to grace, and invited to glory, may persevere in doing good actions; wherefore we have received the letters of the most potent princess and sovereign lady, Mary, by the grace of God, Queen of Scotland, sealed with her seal. . . .

.   .   .   .

" . . Mary, by the Grace of God, Queen of Scotland, to the Reverend Father in Christ; Lord James by the Grace of God and the Apostolic See, Bishop of St Andrews, our dearest cousin, whom we reverence with honour becoming such a Father. Therefore know ye Reverend Father, that for the praise and honour of the Holy Trinity of the ever blessed and glorious Virgin Mary, of St Ninians, the confessor of all the saints and elect of God. We the aforesaid, Mary, with consent and assent of the illustrious Prince, and Lord James our son, the invincible King of Scotland, and in perpetual memory for the salvation of the soul of the late illustrious Prince James, King of Scotland, our late husband of pious memory; likewise for the souls of all the Kings and Queens of Scotland deceased; also for the salvation of the illustrious prince, our son James, the present King of

Provost and Prebendaries. 47

Scotland; for the salvation of our own soul, those of our father and mother, ancestors, and all the sons and daughters succeeding to, and descending from them; and for the salvation of the Reverend Father in Christ, Lord James, Bishop of St Andrews, our dearest cousin; and for the souls of all those whom consanguinity, affinity, or benefits have endeared to us; and of all those whom we have any way offended in this life to whom we are obliged to make satisfaction, and for the souls of all the faithful deceased. We hereby make, constitute, and ordain, and for ever found a Provostry, for a Provost who shall preside in the Government of the College Church, both in respect to the choir and divine worship performed therein; with 8 prebendaries or priests, and 2 boys or clerks, with a sufficient maintenance. . . .

". . . The Provost of the said College shall, for his subsistence, have the Church of Soltre, with the burdens the said Church is subject to—viz., the vicar of the said Church, his pension shall sustain 3 poor persons residing there, and shall keep the Church and ornaments thereof in good repair; and the said Provost shall have the lands of the Barns of Soltre (now Woodcote), and those of the village of Hangingshaw, with their appurtenances, together with the Church of Limpetlaw, with all the fruits, &c. . . .

". . . The first Prebendary shall be called the Master of the Hospital of the Holy Trinity, near Edinburgh, who shall have for the support of this prebend the fourth part of the fruits belonging to the Rectorial Church of Strathmartin; a two pound land in the village of Fawlawhill, below Heriot Moor; an annuity of 2 merks out of the houses in Leith, which belonged to the late William Chines; 20s. Scotch in the village of Risiltone; and 2s. out of the house of John Allansone and John Lawson, in Leith; 20s. annually out of the house of —— Wauk, let in Edinburgh; 5s. yearly out of the house of Thomas, Bishop of Dunkeld; 6s. 8d. in the village of Lawder; 6s. 8d. in the village of Strathmiglo, to be by us declared hereafter, as it is more fully contained in the rental of Soutra; and tenpence out of a certain village near Linlithgow, as is ascertained in the rental; and 5-merks lands of Brotherstanes and Gilstoune, within the Lordship of Soltre, with their limits, marches, and bounds to be hereafter specified. . . .

. . . .

" . . . The second Prebendary shall be called the Sacristan, who, for his support, shall have the 5-merk lands in the village of Hill, within the domain of Balerno; the 5-merk land of Browderstanes and Gilstoune, of the domain of Soutra, to be limited by us, as aforesaid, &c. . . .

. . . .

" . . . The third Prebendary shall be called the Prebendary of Brotherstanes, who shall have for his prebend the 2-merk lands of Brotherstanes and Gilstoune, to be appointed by us, and a fourth part of the profits of the Rectory of Strathmartin.

"The fourth Prebendary shall have for his support the 5-merks lands of Brotherstanes and Gilstoune, and a fourth part of the profits of the Rectory of Strathmartin. . . .

"The fifth Prebendary shall have the title of Gilstoune, and have for his prebend the 5-merk lands of Broderstanes and Gilstoune. . . .

. . . . . .

"The sixth Prebendary, which shall be dominated Ormistoun, shall have the 5-merk lands of Browderstanes and Gilstoune. . . .

. . . . . .

"The seventh Prebendary, to be called of Hill, to have for his prebend the 5-merk lands within the demaine of Balerno. . . .

"The eighth Prebendary, who shall be intitled Newlands, shall for his support have the 5-merk lands of Newlands, in the demaine of Soltre . . . and to uphold the church of Ormistoun by the first fruits arising therefrom, &c."

This charter, as may be understood, stripped the Hospital of its importance as well as its revenues, and the church of the Hospital became the church for the district, which was served by a vicar. The provost and chapter of the new Hospital became the patrons of the vicars in each of the parishes whose churches were under Soutra.

(1.) The first vicar appointed by the Provost and Chapter, after the Monastery was stripped, is styled Dominus Johannes Hyrotte, Vicarius de Soltre; and in 1467 he was witness to several charters.

In October 1479, in a civil action, the Lords of Parliament directed Roby Learmont and others to prove that Sir John Heriot, as Vicar of Soutra, claimed having power from Sir Edward Bonkill, Provost of Trinity College, Edinburgh, to grant a lease of the teinds of Fawnys. His history cannot be traced beyond 1489.

(2.) He was succeeded by Edward Red, of whose history nothing can be found, except that he was witness to several charters.

(3.) John Fidlar, the next vicar, was also witness to charters.

(4.) Thomas Cairns was vicar up to, and for about seven years after, the Reformation. He left to make room for the first Presbyterian minister in 1567, after he had reclaimed some of the property originally belonging to Soutra.

The names of the following Beadsmen and Hospitallers occur in various charters—William Anderson, Robert Hecquat, William Smyth, and Robert Watson. Vicar Pensioners of Soutra—Thomas Bathcat and John Grief.

The transfer to Edinburgh also closed the connection Soutra had with the diocese of St Andrews; and afterwards, when parishes were erected, Soutra was declared by the Pope to be the Parish Church for the district or parish of Soutra.

Under the transfer charter, the Provost, &c., were to bear the burdens incumbent on the Soutra Church, viz., to pay the vicar; to support three poor persons dwelling in the parish; and to keep the church in repair.

The vicar was paid, the church and other ecclesiastical buildings were kept in repair up the Reformation, but no trace of the payments made to the poor can be found after a few years.

Under the reign of Queen Mary, in 1566, a grant was made to the Lord Provost and Magistrates of Edinburgh of the charge of the Hospital; and on the 25th April 1585, a contract was entered into by Pont, the provost of the Trinity College Hospital, for 300 merks, on the receipt of which he was to resign the provostship, and also the parish kirk, parsonage, and vicarage of Soutra, Limpetlaw, and other kirks and teinds annexed to the said Provestrie. The Crown

Beadsman's Acres.   51

confirmed this in May 1587. Although this charter is important, as it gives an account of the property possessed, &c., it is silent regarding the three Soutra beadsmen, or even the payments made to them. About the same period an action was raised at the instance of the two of the three Hospitallaris (Beadsmen) of Sowtray, who had obtained a decree on the 20th February 1583-4, regarding the four acres of land, houses, biggins, and perten thairof, pertaining to the said persawaris as Hospitallaris foresaidis lands in Sowtray hill. The action was fallen from, and nothing came out of it. It is supposed, and supposed upon good grounds, that this said lands (four acres) were the acres that James V. gave as a grant to the Pringles, of the Beadsman's Acres, for a night's shelter. Father Hay, in his " Scota Sacra," a MS. of great historical interest in the Advocates' Library, says "that James V., in 1542, collected about 30,000 soldiers from all parts of the country, and ordered them to be gathered at Soutra hill." It is supposed that the king had visited the district about this time, and had lost himself in the woods, which at that time covered the greater part of the Lammermuirs. He at last came upon the house occupied by one John Pringle, the shepherd for the district under Sir William Borthwick. The king requested shelter for the night, never revealing his person; but the pauky herd, conscious of the rank of his guest, asked him in, and directed the guidwife to take down the hen which sat next to the cock on the baulks and roast it for the stranger's supper.

The King supped and retired for the night, and was so much pleased in the morning with the kind hospitality which he received, that he made Pringle a gift of the lands of the

Beadsmen's Acres, which were to be held by him and his successors for all time coming. The Pringles held possession of this land to the beginning of this century, when it was purchased by the laird of Soutra Mains, whose lands surround it. This ground was situated west from the Isle, and on the south of the road that leads to Gilston. The Pringles lived in a small house on the Beadman's Acres, which disappeared shortly before these lands were sold. A ballad was composed by some one, and sung by itinerants during the last decade of last century, entitled, " The gudewife of Soutra," but all that can now be found is the following—

> " Hae ye no heard o' the gude auld times,
> When Pringle was sae luckie,
> To get a lump o' Soutrahill,
> Just for a roasted chuckie."

CHAPTER VII.

LANDS OF SOUTRA.

Soutra Lands — Soutra Beacons — The Hertford Invasion — "Surety Men" — Hunter's Hall — Lawrie's Den — Soutra Witch — Mr John Ainslie — The Deil's Putting Stone.

ALTHOUGH the oldest charter speaks of the lands around the Monastery of Soutra as a "gift" from Malcolm the Maiden, in all likelihood the Master and Brethren were in possession long before; and the charter only confirming that which they already possessed. In this ancient document there are no names of previous owners, as in the other charters, the omission of which tacitly acknowledges their ownership. As common at the times, "lands and men" were all included in their possession. As far as can be learned, that land which they at first possessed came, when parishes were defined, to be called the parish of Soutra, East Lothian. Why this tongue of land, lying between Mid-Lothian and Berwickshire, should be declared as East Lothian must ever remain an unanswered question? In agricultural value, the contrast between this parish and Fala is striking. Fala is generally 150 feet below the level of Soutra, yet Soutra is, and ever has been, in a much higher state of cultivation, owing largely to the activity of the monks. The parish has no moorland; and has been divided into five different properties, viz., Soutra proper, Gilston, Over and Nether Brotherstone, and a small part of Johnstonburn on the east, called Kelly-bauk.

As Watling Street of the Romans, the King's Road, made in the time of Malcolm, and the present road of 1834,—all run through this *property*, and as from the summit there is such a commanding view of the Lothians, it became famous, in a strategical way, during the invasion of the English. There is much historical matter in this connection which must ever remain unknown, yet often *telegraphic* communications by beacon and faggot were made with Edinburgh to the north, and the Eildons to the south.

By an Act of Parliament in 1455, one bale or faggot was to be a warning of the approach of the English in any manner; two, that they are coming indeed; and four, beside each other, that they are coming in great force. Those at Hume were to signal to those at Eggerhope Castle, " and those on Soutra Edge shall see the fire of Eggerhope Castle, and make taiking in like manner, and then may all Lothian be warned."

In 1588, when panic had seized the whole country over the Spanish Armada, the Privy Council of Scotland appointed Commissioners under Earl Bothwell "to cause baillis to be brynt and watcheis kepit at all placis and occasions requisite—St Abb's Head, Hume Castle, Eldon Hills, Soutrahill, North Berwick Law, &c."

Even so far down as at the beginning of this century these signals were used to communicate warlike intelligence. During the alarm caused by Napoleon's victories and threatened invasion, Soutra Edge was seen to be on fire. The last beacon that was lit was not the signal to arms, but of a more peaceful and joyous character. In 1887, when Queen Victoria's jubilee was being celebrated, the people of Soutrahill joined with her loyal subjects everywhere in giving expression to their feelings of devotion and respect. The hill-tops around were on fire as of old, and the blaze on Soutrahill was conspicuous among the many, lasting far over the night. The dying embers, as seen from below, blown by the evening gale, cast a lurid glimmer over the young mountain grass, and brought to mind with feelings of romance the couplet of Sir Walter Scott in the " Romance of Sir Tristem," which says—

> " In deepening mass, at distance seen,
> Broad Soltre's mountains lay."

The people of Soutra suffered during the Hertford invasion. In 1542 the lairds and people were harassed by the presence of the army of the Earls Seton, Home, and Buccleuch, who were stationed at Soutra, and whose wants had to be supplied from the neighbouring farms. But this did not end their troubles, for, as they looked round during the presence of the army, they saw the fertile plains of Merse and Lothian and the Metropolis itself reduced to a smoking desert, a fate that was soon to befall themselves. In January 1544, Captain John Ker came with " the number of 9 scoir men and burnt Soutray and Fawlaw and thereafter the lairds of the county followed them and took 24 men."

Hertford the same year returned to England by Soutra after burning several villages in Fife and around Edinburgh. He marched southwards burning, slaying, and ruining as he went. In October of this same year Lord Angus, who had been on attendance on Queen Mary at Jedburgh, rode to Soutra to disperse a few English who came from Kirkton, capturing all they met.

In 1547, the English army returned by Fala and Soutrahill, after they had taken Hume Castle, Fast Castle, and the town of Haddington. These incidents show that Soutra was a convenient route between Edinburgh and the south. But it was also a convenient meeting-place for the armies of the Lothians. King James in 1588 issued a proclamation that all the earls, barons, lords, freeholders, and substantious gentlemen dwelling within the bounds of the shire of Edinburgh, Haddington, and Peebles, were to meet his highness at Soutra upon the 18th April, and go with him to reduce the disturbance on the West Marches.

The Privy Council looked upon Soutra as the *ultima thule* of the Lothians when they were receiving surety from the lairds for military service and other causes.

The following are some of the curious entries in their records:—

"1544. The Rutherfords, Turnbulls, and Cranstouns, to remain within the Castle of Edinburgh till 10th February. If any of them wish to relieve their sureties that they shall obey the laws of Scotland or England (they and their followers to keep good rule), they shall find sureties (inlanded men sufficient within Soutra Edge)."

"January 2nd, 1593. William Borthwick of Johnstoun and Soutra, as principal, and Patrick Murray of Fala Hill, Sheriff of Selkirk, as surety, £1000, not to harm Robert Oliphant of Aulderstoune, burgess of Edinburgh."

"July 1595. William Borthwick of Johnstoun and Soutra, for George, Earl of Mairshall, 5000 merks, not to harm James Lawson of Humbie."

"September 1598. William Borthwick of Johnstoun and Soutra, for Margaret Borthwick, relict of Robert Lauder of

WOODCOTE PARK (EAST FRONT).

that Ilk, 300 merks, to deliver the fortalice of Lauder, which belonged before to her late husband, to William Lauder of Cauldshiels, in case it should be found she ought to do so."

The village was restored after its destruction in 1544, and existed up to the end of last century, although now not a single stone stands to mark its site. It is supposed to have stood on the flat, the centre of which was the Isle and old church-yard. It grew to considerable dimensions, for one of the ministers speaks of it as having several public-houses. Near the village, to the south, was the King's Inch or common lands, consisting of several acres, but these now have fallen into the possession of Mr Borthwick of Crookston, and are held to be in the parish of Channelkirk, County of Berwick. On the flat of the hill, on the right of the "King's Road," stood a large house called Hunter's Hall. It was used as a meeting place for various sportsmen, and when the country lairds were given more to fox-hunting than they are at the present, a pack of hounds was kept there for their amusement. On the opposite side of the road—the east side—was situated a well-known public-house, which was possessed for a considerable time by a family named Lawrie. It was conveniently situated for drovers, carters, and carriers, and was often the scene of many a quarrel and bloody fight. About eighty years ago the gipsies, who were encamped on the common, or King's Inch, had been drinking freely at Lawrie's Den, the name by which it is best known. A quarrel arose, and one was killed; another was captured, tried, and hanged for the offence, and some others were imprisoned for a time. All that now remains of this public-house are a few lines of doggerel which were painted on a signboard at the door, and which are remembered by some of the oldest inhabitants.

> "Humpty, dumpty, heerie, peerie;
> Step in here and ye'll be cheerie.
> Try oor speerits an' oor porter,
> They'll make the road the shorter.
> And if ye hae a mind to stay,
> Your horse can get guid corn and hay.
> Good entertainment for man and horse."

About 600 yards north from Lawrie's Den, and about 200 yards to the east of the public road, stood for many a long day a turf hut, and occupied last by an old woman named Margaret Dobson. Margaret for long, by her strange retiring habits, was a terror to the neighbourhood, and as there was a halo of the "unearthly" thrown around her, she was blamed for every evil that befell any one in the district. If a storm suddenly arose from the south, Margaret was blamed. If sudden death came to a home or to any of the cattle, Margaret had her hand in it. If bad harvest weather came, Margaret was the cause—in short, she was feared and dreaded as a witch, and was considered to be in league with the powers of darkness. Margaret lived to the age of ninety, and died about forty years ago.

Mr John A. Ainslie, nephew of Mr Ainslie, the respected proprietor of Costerton, after his father's death lived with his uncle at Costerton. He was educated at Harrow and at Oxford, where he graduated with honours; but as he had undermined his health with over-study, he died at Algiers, where he had gone to recruit himself, on the 12th March 1874. His relatives put into the English church at Algiers

John A. Ainslie.

a beautiful stained glass window to his memory. John Ainslie loved to roam over Soutrahill, and became so familiar with the story of Margaret Dobson, that when at Harrow School he wrote the following narrative of her.

Standing on Soutrahill, he says—

"Once as I gazed, a sad mysterious wail
Came gently stealing on the autumn gale;
Low, mournful, thrilling, then a bitter sigh,
Which chilled me to the heart, I scarce knew why.
It seemed in low-breathed accents thus to say,
'A few short hours, and might resume her sway.'
Sudden I turn, there crouching close behind,
Her long grey locks loose streaming in the wind,
Sits a weird woman. O'er her snowy head
Full more than fourscore winters must have fled:
Yet something tells that care as well as age
Hath left its traces on her life's dark page,
Hath ploughed that withered cheek with many a seam,
And lit in that dark eye a maniac gleam.
Awestruck I watched her, with suspended breath,
So still she sat, so like a living death,
Whence hath she come? What can this spectre be?
Some weak delusion! Some mock fantasy!
Thus vainly combating my rising fear,
I see close by, grim, solitary, drear—

"The aisle of a deserted church, which crowned
The topmost summit of a grassy mound,
And still preserved from sacrilegious tread,
The resting place of the forgotten dead;
Telling, that even here for a brief span
Had lived, and rioted, and perished, man.
Abandoned now, with those who in it sleep,
To the lone visits of the mountain sheep.

Fala and Soutra.

But hark! A shrill, protracted, echoing cry,
As wrung from some doomed spirit's agony,
Breaks the calm stillness of the morning air,
Proclaiming that still *she* is lingering there;
No more low cowering, no more bound or still,
But tall, erect, as one foreboding ill
To all who hapless fall beneath the blaze
Of that ill-omened, fury-flashing gaze.
Silent she stood, then tossed her arms on high,
And thus commenced with horrid mystery.

"Strange fitful murmurs fill my listening ears,
My boding heart beats high with unknown fears,
Hushed is all nature's voice; some mighty spell
Hangs o'er the mouutain, hovers in the dell,
While inborn voices speak with every breath
Of vengeance, ruin, swift approaching death.
Hence, mortals, hence forsake the field and wood,
Nor tempt by lingering, the angry God.
For soon I tell ye, shall the Prince of Wrath
Triumphant ride the raging Forth,
Wrap in his gloomy pall these hills, and roll
His fiery thunderbolts from pole to pole;
Mark, how e'en now on Lammerlaw's proud form
Broods the dark genius of the impending storm,
Waiting the signal to swoop down and pour
His noisome vapours on this smiling shore.
    Ha! Ha! I see it rise,
    Lowering in the distant skies,
    It comes, it comes, and with it brings
    Destruction seated on its wings;
    Hark! I hear a dismal groaning,
    Rising, falling, sighing, moaning,
    While a warning voice is there
    Bidding all the world prepare.
    Haste then, haste thou furious blast,

JOHN A. AINSLIE, M.A., OXON.

Deil's Putting Stone.

>   Drive the stormcloud, drive it fast;
>   Tremble mortals, shake, but I
>   With those who here forgotten lie,
>   Bursting from the open tomb
>   Revel in the midnight gloom
>   'Neath the mirky veil of night,
>   Or the moonbeams' struggling light:
>   While the tempest gathers o'er us,
>   And the lightning flash before us,
>   Raise a loud and hideous chorus
>   To the sky.'
>
> She ceased exhausted with her mystic lay,
> Then raised her arms, and shrieked, and fled away."

Until recently, there stood nicely poised on the top of the rock overlooking the Linndean Waterfall, a large boulder of about twenty tons weight, called the "Deil's putting stone." Tradition has it that his Satanic Majesty was on the "spree" at Carfrae Inn, and got into a dispute about putting stones with some handloom weavers from Lauder. A bet was taken that he could putt the boulder clear over the Lammermuirs. An attempt was made, but it only reached the Linndean Waterfall, where it had lain for ages. The Deil, true to his nature, refused to pay the bet, and the moral now is, " Never bet with the Deil."

CHAPTER VIII.

PROPRIETORS OF SOUTRA.

The Geology — William Borthwick — Robert Fletcher — Pringles — Maitlands—Reidhall—Falconers—Sir Thomas Napier—Mrs Ogilvie—Woodcote—Lord Wood—Lord Justice General Inglis—Mr Lothian—Mr Crombie—Mr Horn—Gilston Tower—Proprietors of Gilston—N. Brotherstones and Proprietors—Andersons of Whitburgh—Kellybaak and Johnstounburn Proprietors—Keith Marischal.

THE geology of the upper part of Soutra is almost similar to that which is found over the greater part of the Lammermuirs—an inferior whin, and on the lower part that of the lower red sandstone, which is a good specimen of a building stone. Hematite ironstone has been found in the streams, and when analysed has been found to contain about 82 per cent. of pure iron. Limestone was burnt, and clay was dug for brickmaking, until both were found to be not worth the labour spent in getting them.

Unless the various Prebendaries of Trinity College, Edinburgh, farmed themselves the different properties from which their respective incomes came, there is now no account of tack or lease of proprietor or tenant until after the Reformation.

When King James, in 1587, confirmed the charter granting the church lands of Soutra to the Burgh of Edinburgh, the Town Council entered into a tack with William Borthwick for nineteen years, at the yearly rent of £30 Scots.

This William Borthwick was the son of another William Borthwick of Soutra Mains, who may have been the steward

William Borthwick.   63

or grieve upon the place before. Under this tack, which is the first that is recorded, he was to uphold also the parish kirk of Soutra " by sufficiently bigging, besting, mending, repairing, and upholding; the town's share being one-third of the whole." The Borthwicks were in possession also of Johnstounburn, and these lands they possessed until the year 1650, when they passed by marriage to Robert Fletcher, connected with the Saltoun family. It is curious that all the Borthwicks whose names are extant were surnamed William. They built, shortly after possession, the old mansion called " Meusdenhead," which means the head of the den where hawking was practised in olden times. This mansion was situated in what is now known as the " Barnyard Park," and the approach from the present lodge runs in a straight line to its site. Some time ago the old foundations were dug up when draining the field. The Borthwicks were also the first to build a house upon Johnstonburn, where they afterwards went to reside. In 1608, William Borthwick having failed to appear as charged, to answer for the reset of thieves, stolen goods, rebels, and horners in the house of Johnstoun, and for airt and pairt with them, is to be denounced a rebel. He became also surety for £1000 not to harm George Hepburne of Elstaneford. Robert Fletcher and

Lord Wood's Coat of Arms above front door.

his son and heir, Andrew, who held the property for twenty years, paid a yearly feu-duty to the Town Council of 7s. The property returns again to the Borthwicks, who had it for five years, when by marriage it passes into the hands of the Pringles, who were in possession for thirty years. In 1700, Charles Maitland, a member of the Lauderdale family, appears as proprietor; then David in 1717; another Charles in 1720, who built the old part of the present mansion, and called it Reidhall; and lastly, Lieutenant Thomas Maitland, who died in 1773. His daughter married a Mr Falconer, who became proprietor; and her brother got as his share Pogbie, which up to this time was a part of the estate. The Maitlands were in Pogbie up to thirty years ago, when the last died, who was named David. He was quite a character. When dying he carefully instructed his butler, and sister's sons, who were his heirs, to bury him in the family vaults of the Isle, which they retained with the Pogbie property. They were also to lock the door, and to throw into the vault the keys, to prevent anyone from having access thereto. This was literally carried out. The nephew, Charles Maitland Keith, is the present owner.

Thomas Falconer, as proprietor of Reidhall and Soutra Mains, was succeeded by his son Alexander, who changed the name of the estate into Woodcote Park, to commemorate the erection of the present hedges of beech and hawthorn; and also the laying out of the present woods in 1791. He died in 1795, and was buried in Fala Churchyard, where a marble mural tablet was erected to his memory. He left a son, George Home Falconer, and three daughters. George, when quite a lad, joined the Scots Greys, and by his distinguished services at Waterloo, was promoted to the position of captain.

Woodcote Park.   65

Shortly afterwards he retired, married, and settled at Woodcote, to fill the position of a worthy father. But providence had decreed that his life should be short upon earth, for after a severe cold, which seized him in the spring of 1820, he died in September of the same year, and was buried beside his parents. A white marble mural tablet was erected in the Church to his memory, bearing the following :—

Sacred to the memory of
GEORGE HOME FALCONER, Esq., of Woodcote;
late Captain in the Scots Greys,
A Justice of the Peace in the county of Haddington,
and an Elder in this Parish,
who departed this life on the 15th Sept., 1820,
in the thirtieth year of his age.
This tablet is placed with lasting affection and respect
by his deeply afflicted widow.
" Shall we receive good at the hand of the Lord,
and shall we not receive evil."
" The Lord gave, and the Lord hath taken
away : blessed be the name of the Lord !"

One of his three sisters died shortly afterwards, another married Lieut.-Colonel T. E. Napier of Thirlstane, brother to Admiral Napier of India fame, and got as a dowry the property which is now known as Woodcote Park. He was an elder in the parish for several years. The other sister married the late Mr Ogilvie of Chesters, Ancrum, and got as her portion Soutra Mains. Mrs Ogilvie lived to a great age, and died three years ago at Chesters. Her son, Thomas Elliot Ogilvie, is now the proprietor of Soutra Mains.

Colonel Napier, who became Sir Thomas E. Napier, lived in and possessed Woodcote for eighteen years; and in

1843 sold it to Thomas Griffies Dixon. Mr Dixon married, and several children were born to him before he left in 1854 for Nant Hall, Wales, where he presently resides. Woodcote was destined to become more famous by having for its owner Lord Wood, one of the Senators of the College of Justice. Immediately, whenever the property was purchased, he employed Bryce, the famous Edinburgh architect, who, by his genius and skill, transformed a square, plain country house into a fine Scottish baronial mansion. Lord Wood not only enlarged the house, but he also made walks, erected little chalets and bowers; and planted as fine a selection of shrubbery as may be found in the Lothians. He also acquired from Mrs Ogilvie, in 1857, the ground around the well-known Linndean Waterfall, and thereby added variety and character to his summer retreat. Woodcote appeared under Lord Wood at its best. He took great interest in not only adding beauty to beauty, but in keeping everything about his grounds and woods and fields in the finest order. He was much respected in the parish and district; and his house was always well filled with guests and friends during his vacation. He also took a fatherly interest in the poor, and in the affairs of the parish generally. By his influence and exertion he got the present Parish Church rebuilt. In 1864, after a residence of ten years, he died at Woodcote, and was buried in the family vault at Restalrig. His widow put stained glass into the three east windows of the Church, which have the following inscription :—" Dedicated by his widow to the memory of Alexander Wood of Woodcote, born 13th November 1788, died 19th July 1864." He left a large family of sons and daughters. One of the daughters married, in 1842, John

Gilstoun.

Inglis, who became Lord Justice-General, one of the greatest men who ever presided over the Supreme Courts of Scotland. He died 20th August, 1891, several years after his wife. Another daughter married Dr Wilson, who has carried on a very successful medical practice in Florence for many years. After Lord Wood's death the property fell into the hands of John Anderson Wood, his eldest son. Mr John Wood was a distinguished student of Edinburgh University. He became an Advocate, but soon afterwards fell into delicate health, and was invalid until his death in May 1890, one year and three months before his distinguished brother-in-law. He sold the property in 1874 to Mr M. J. Lothian, who made it famous for its game preserves. Mr Lothian, after seven years proprietorship, sold it to Mr Crombie of Thornton Castle, Laurencekirk, who again sold it in 1891 to Mr Horn, Advocate, a distinguished Oxford student. Very few places in Scotland have passed through so many hands, and have had such a variety of owners as Woodcote. It is to be hoped that the present respected proprietor and his posterity will possess it for generations.

The fine pasture lands of Gilston lie immediately to the west of Soutra Hill. It has been the common belief that Gilston got its name from one of its owners, named Gill, who bequeathed his lands to Soutra Monastery. But for this there is not to be found the slightest foundation. The first time the name appears is in connection with a confirmation charter by King Alexander II., confirming the possession of the lands by the Monastery. This old Latin charter gives it as Gilliestoun, which may mean the town of the gillies or servants of the Monastery. This is the most likely derivation, as the monks would have stationed there for agricultural purposes a staff of men. Gillstoun, like Woodcote, Soutra Hill, and the Brotherstones, is held in feu from the Town Council of Edinburgh. Woodcote and Soutra paid as feu-duty £2, 10s. per year; a part of Soutra Hill, 2s. 2½d.; Kellybaak (Johnstounburn), 8s. 4½d.; Nether Brotherstone, £1, 2s. 2½d.; Over Brotherstone, £1, 2s. 2½d.; and Gillstoun the same per year. All these feu-duties, according to the wish of the Town Council, were bought up by the respective proprietors in 1827 for twenty-five years' purchase. Gillstoun still pays 5s. yearly to the Marquis of Tweeddale as feu-duty; but it is for a small piece of land which belonged to the Tweeddale property, and which was acquired by the Gillstoun owner, as it was surrounded by his lands. Upon this piece of land stood an old house until a few years ago, which went by the name of "Mak' him rich," a name which was applied by the inhabitants owing to the easy terms of its possession.

Gillstoun is of some historical interest to the antiquary, as there is still standing in the centre of the property an old peel tower. Of its origin, history, or object, nothing is known beyond the fact that it existed prior to the Reformation, at which time it was repaired by the proprietor. It may have had its origin in the time of the Romans, as it would command the approach from the west to Watling Street, or it may have been erected by the monks for a similar purpose. All that now remains has been transformed into dwelling-houses for the workmen on the property.

About three-quarters of a mile to the west of the tower are still to be found the foundations of an old Roman camp, of which there are several in the neighbourhood.

GILSTOUN TOWER.

Brotherstones. 69

Nothing, so far as is known, has been done to excavate in search of relics, or even to know its extent or shape.

Gillstoun has had several proprietors since it fell into the hands of the Edinburgh Town Council, through the Trinity College Hospital. The first that is recorded who got a feu of the lands of Gilston and Over Brotherstone, is James Abernethy. He held them from 1549. Sir William Seton of Cakemuir is proprietor from 1620 to 1656, when he sold them to Sir Alexander Auchmutie of Gosford, who sold them again to Alexander Elphinstoun in 1694. In 1707 they were sold to Thomas Baillie, a merchant in Musselburgh, whose heirs sold them in 1774 to Thomas Bervie. Early this century they were purchased by Robert Brown of Musselburgh, who sold them in 1850 to the late John Dun, merchant, Leith. They are now held by Mr Dun's trustee, and are farmed by Mr Dun's only son, who becomes proprietor. Mr Dun improved the value of the property by draining and fencing; and of late the cottages have been so much improved, that they are now the finest workmen's cottages in the parish.

Nether Brotherstones is the south-western point of the parish, and derives its name, like Upper Brotherstones, from the stony nature of the soil. From the fact that it is called Brotherstones in the first charters extant, shows that the Brethren of the Monastery had been long in possession when the lands were called by their name. There is nothing of historical interest connected with this small property of about 120 acres, except the site of two old Roman camps, one of which is completely obliterated; the other shows a slight elevation above the surrounding soil. The Armit, which rises in the Hen's Moss opposite Lawrie's Den on the Lauder road, flows past the Cross Chain Hill, the King's Inch, Mak' him rich, Gilston, and forms the south boundary of Nether Brotherstones, whence it proceeds to Crookstone, where it joins the Gala. The Armet is one of the finest trouting streams in the district. The Brothershiels burn, which flows from Fala Moor, forms the boundary on the north and west.

Of the proprietors little is known. The first who appears is Alexander Hodge, who held the property until it passed into the hands of the Andersons of Whitburgh, in the parish of Humbie, about the year 1680. The Andersons possessed it until about 1850, when it was sold to William Paterson, lawyer, Edinburgh; and his heirs sold it to Robert Young, merchant, Ratho, whose widow is in present possession. The Andersons, although living in another parish, took all along a warm interest in the welfare of the parish. They had acquired the lands of Whitburgh from James Calderwood, minister of Humbie, who got a gift of them from Charles II., and also was presented to the living of Humbie Parish because he adopted Episcopacy. The Hepburnes of Humbie were the old proprietors, who lost them owing to their strong loyal leanings for "Christ, Kirk, and Covenant." The Andersons sold Whitburgh in 1877 to Charles Watson of Glasgow, who sold it again to Mr Slimon in 1885, the present proprietor, who is one of the most hospitable of men.

Kellybaak, a small part of the estate of Johnstounburn, forms the eastern part of the parish of Soutra, in East Lothian. Kellybaak is a contraction for Kelly's baak, the baak or baulk of Kelly, who lived in a small house in that land about the middle of last century. Soutra Croft, or Kiln Croft is the proper name. Johnstounburn, as given to the House of

Johnstounburn.

Soutra by John Marishall de Keith, included also the two fields that surround the present farm house of Upper Keith, the property of Mr Usher. The Frasers were the original proprietors of the western districts of East Lothian, possessing Johnstounburn, Humbie, Upper and Lower Keith, Whitburgh, and Costerton. A daughter of Simon Fraser married Keith Symm or Philip de Keith, and took to her husband Keith Harvey and Keith Hundley. "Hundley" after a time became "Humbie," which has been a parish since the Reformation, and includes both the properties designated under "Keith." The Master and Brethren farmed these "gifted" lands up to the time of the transfer to Edinburgh in 1462. The Provost and Prebendaries of the Trinity College, Edinburgh, would in all likelihood let them to tenants until the Reformation, when the Town Council, representing the Trinity College, took possession. Like the other lands of Soutra, they were let as a feu to the Borthwicks, who were in possession to 1659, when Helen, daughter of the late Thomas Borthwick, married James Primrose, a soldier, and was served heir. She died in 1687, and left the property to her husband. Primrose retained it till about the year 1730, when it was purchased by Thomas Crocket, merchant, Edinburgh. Crocket was for a number of years Dean of Guild, and died about 1770, when he bequeathed 10,000 merks to the poor of Edinburgh, as well as some other gifts. At that time it was purchased by the ancestors of the present proprietor, Archibald Brown, who was primus clerk to the Court of Session for a great number of years. Johnstounburn is finely wooded, and laid out, like Woodcote, with great taste and expense, which makes it a charming residential property.

The old house that was built by the Borthwicks on the west side of the stream, which comes from Woodcote, was enlarged and improved at considerable expense several years ago. The old farm house, called Chesterhill, was also enlarged, and is now the residence of Mr Brown and family; and a very fine house at the steading was erected for the farm tenant.

FALA KIRK.

CHAPTER IX.

CHURCH OF FALA.

Fala Church—Furnishings—Communion Cups—Bell—Churchyard—Mort Cloth—Fala Manse—Glebe—Patronage—Right of Presentation, Sale of——.

AFTER 1462 the church of Soutra became a vicarage church, and remained in that condition until the Reformation, when the first Presbyterian minister entered in, and carried on religious worship in the same building that had been used by the last Roman Catholic vicar.

This church, no doubt a part of the old church of the Monastery, was in use for public worship up to 1624, when the parish minister removed to the church and manse in Fala village.

The Fala church at the Reformation had suffered violence at the hands of the people, as the priest had fled, and would not conform to the new order. It stood in this condition till the year 1591, when it was put into repair, and used for one year as the parish church. After the removal of the minister to Soutra village, the church stood unused until 1624, when he got it repaired. From that date up to 1861 it was continuously used as the church of the two parishes. In 1861, greatly through the influence of the late Lord Wood of Woodcote, Mr Bryce, R.S.A., Edinburgh, was engaged to prepare plans of a new church. He recommended that the new church should be erected upon the site and foundations of the old, which was ultimately carried out.

The old foundations were used, the church was made the same shape and size of the old, the only omission being the chancel, which may be supplied at some future time. The pulpit was placed against the east wall instead of the south, where it formerly stood; and there is only one gallery, which is against the west wall, instead of the two which were in the old building. It is now one of the prettiest and most comfortable of our rural parish churches.

While the church was being rebuilt, a very interesting discovery was made in the shape of a flat tombstone, upon which the only legible words were—

    . . . . Nairne . . of . Dunsinnane . . .

It is matter of regret that means were not adopted at the time the stone was laid bare to decipher the remaining part of the inscription, as some light might have been given to assist in clearing up an epoch in the history of the Nairne family.

As the church was in continuous use from the time of its repair in 1624, and as an Act of the General Assembly prohibited burials in churches, this burial must have taken place prior to that date. About the year 1600 there were two Nairnes, Sir William and Sir Thomas. After the death of the former, the latter got into trouble, left his residence at Dunsinnane, and wandered about from place to place. He must have wandered to Fala, and probably may have taken up his residence in Fala Hall, the house of the Hays and Edmonstones, and, having died, was buried in Fala Church. At the east end of the church, and directly under what was called the Stair or Hamilton gallery, were also found the remains of one of Lord Stair's ancestors.

Communion Vessels. 75

In this case, as in the other, nothing was done to satisfy curiosity or the desire of original research.

The two brass candelabra, which hang from the ceiling of the church, are supposed to be all that remains of the pre-Reformation times. Men skilled in metal work, who have examined them, consider that they are of Belgian origin, and that they may have been made prior to 1560. As some information about the other property of the Church exists, and as the Roman catholic priest officiated up to the time of the appointment of the first Presbyterian minister, these candelabra may have been left behind, and may have been brought from Soutra to Fala in 1624.

The common iron frame of the old sand-glass, and of the baptismal font, which are fixed in front of the present pulpit, were made about 1650; a new sand-glass was bought in 1678, which cost eight shillings Scots.

The two solid silver communion cups are of considerable value. They are shaped like a modern champagne glass, and were made in Edinburgh about the year 1600. As the assayers' books for that period are lost, this date is given as the most probable. They were exhibited in the Edinburgh Exhibition of 1886. The other

Fala Kirk Communion Cup (silver).

Communion plate are of common pewter, and were given to the Church by Thomas Hamilton Macgill de Fala in 1715.

The Kirk Tokens.

In every parish the bell usually plays a very important part: and it so happens that around the bell of Fala a halo of romance has grown, and many stories about it have been told. After inquiry, it turns out that tradition is wrong, that the stories are unworthy of belief, and even of record. The bell belongs properly to Borthwick parish, for which it was made, and made at a time when the rules for grammar were very flexible. How it came to Fala, and at what time, are unanswered questions. Neither the records of the one parish nor the other can give any information. It is most likely a cast-off bell, having been replaced by a larger at Borthwick, and brought here to supply a want. The inscription on it is quaint, and worthy of reproduction.

>I do call to feed sleep and pray
>God bless you all good people of Borthwick
>MDCCXXIX.   you all.

Of the bell it may be said—

>"It's crackit, noo, an' jinglin',
>It's failin' like mysel'—
>Yet weel I lo'e the jowin'
>O' oor ain kirk-bell!
>
>"A handfu's i' the kirk, where ance
>The countryside itsel'
>Wad gaither at the jowin'
>O' oor ain kirk-bell."

Fala Churchyard.

According to a time-honoured custom, the sacred dead lie buried around the place consecrated to the worship of God. As neither tradition nor history gives the slightest idea of another place of sepulture in the parish, there can be no doubt that the churchyard around the parish church of Fala has existed from time immemorial. Alas! like too many of our rural churchyards, its condition is a reproach, and its walls are a ruin. Beyond several of the parish ministers, and one or two lairds, nobody, as far as is known, has been buried in it of any note. According to the custom of the past generation, the tombstones bear those emblems of Time, Decay, and Eternity, which are generally adopted.

At Soutra the parishioners at the Reformation changed their manner of worship, but not their churchyard. About one acre or more of the land around the Isle was the burial place for that parish up to the end of last century, when the custom began of burying in Fala Churchyard alone. The walls have all been removed — the very tombstones have disappeared, which the late Dr Laing described as a gross act of vandalism; and now the plough has eaten in year by year, until only a small piece of the old churchyard remains. There has also accumulated on the south side of the Isle a large heap of gathered stones, which gives the place a look of sad neglect.

The mort cloth was in use in the parish up to thirty years ago, when it entirely ceased to be used. For a time there were two, one for the loan of which was paid the sum of five shillings, and the other two shillings and sixpence,—the sexton getting six pence or one shilling for carrying it to the house. The mort cloth dues were paid into the poor box. The good old custom still prevails in the parish, of everybody who can attending the funerals. Often there may be seen quite a crowd of respectably dressed men, from the laird to the hind, walking silently and reverently after the remains of even a child to its last resting-place. Rich and poor lie together.

> " Lay the one great and rich in the strong cloister niche,
> Give him his coffin of cedar and gold ;
> Let the wild torchlight fall, flouting the velvet pall,
> Lock him in marble vault, darksome and cold.
>
> " But there's a sunny hill, fondly remembered still ;
> Crowned with fair grass, and a bonny elm tree ;
> There the wind, loud and strong, whistles its winter song ;
> There spring the wild flowers—fair as can be."

As far as can be ascertained, the priest's house or manse ever occupied the site of the present Fala Manse. After a long struggle, and considerable trouble on the part of the minister, the present manse was built in 1792. It was repaired and enlarged in 1832, and again, after another struggle and some trouble, in 1889, when the " Precentor's Tower " was also erected. It never was a good house, and its present condition clearly indicates that it never will. Complaints shortly after its erection were made against it to the Presbytery ; even its description in the Statistical Account of Parishes in 1793-94 has been verified again and again. . . . The minister at the Reformation occupied the house that the Soutra Vicar left, which was situated on the north side of the road, which passes the Isle. The ministers lived there until 1624, when a removal was made to Fala. Around the Soutra Manse was the glebe of about eight imperial acres, which were excambed to Fala in 1865;

making a glebe of thirteen imperial acres of the best land in the parish.

The patronage of the Church of Fala continued with the Lords of the Manor from the 12th century to the time Patronage was abolished by Act of Parliament in 1872. There are recorded as exercising the right: Dominus Bartholomew de Fala, D. Georgius de Fala, and the Hays, before the Reformation; and the Edmonstones, the Hamiltons, Dalrymple, and Stair, since the Reformation.

From the depletion of the Monastery in 1462 to the Reformation, the Provost and Prebends of the Trinity College, Edinburgh held the Patronage of the Kirk of Soutra, and when the Lord Provost and Magistrates of Edinburgh got possession of the Trinity College, with all its revenues, shortly after the Reformation, they also got the right to present the minister to Soutra. When the two parishes were united in 1618, the Town Council of Edinburgh and the proprietor of Fala became alternate patrons. The following is a copy of the *presentation* made by the Town Council of Edinburgh:—

"Edinburgh, 27th February, 1760.—.... A presentation was this day read and signed in Council, of which the tenor follows:—

"We, George Drummond, Esquire, Lord Provost of the City of Edinburgh; David Flint, Adam Fairholm, Gilbert Lawrie, Robert Selkrig, Bailies; John Carmichael, Dean of Gild; and James Guthrie, Treasurer; together with the remnant Council and Deacons of Crafts, ordinary and extraordinary, of the said City, for ourselves, and as representing the whole body and community thereof, undoubted Patrons of the Parochine and Parish Kirk of Falla, within the Presbytery of Dalkeith, considering that the said Kirk of Falla is at present vacant in our hands, and at our gift and presentation, by the transportation of the Reverend Mr Patrick Simpson, late minister thereof, to the Parish of Cluny, and we being desirous that the same be provided with some well qualified and godly man fitted for the exercise of the Holy Ministry, and being informed of the ability, literature, and qualifications of Mr William Wotherspoon, preacher of the Gospel, to discharge the office and function of a minister within the Church of God, and of the great pains, travel, and study taken by him these several years past for that effect; therefore we have nominated and presented, and by these presents, nominate and present the said Mr William Wotherspoon to the ministry of the said Parochine and Parish Kirk of Falla, and to the manse, glebe, and stipend, with all the privileges, profits, and emoluments of the same as was formerly possest and paid to the said Mr Patrick Simpson, late minister thereof, and that for the croft and year of God one thousand seven hundred and sixty years, and yearly in all times coming during his encumbency there; requiring and hereby desiring the Reverend Moderator and remnant brethren of the said Presbytery of Dalkeith to take trial of his literature and qualifications, and being found qualified, to admit him to the said Church, conform to the rules of ecclesiastical discipline, established by law and order, used in such cases. In witness whereof (written on stamped paper by John Forbes, servitor to the principal city clerks of Edinburgh), We the said Lord Provost, Bailies, Dean of Gild, and Treasurer, as also Mr William Forbes, one of the City Clerks, in name and at the

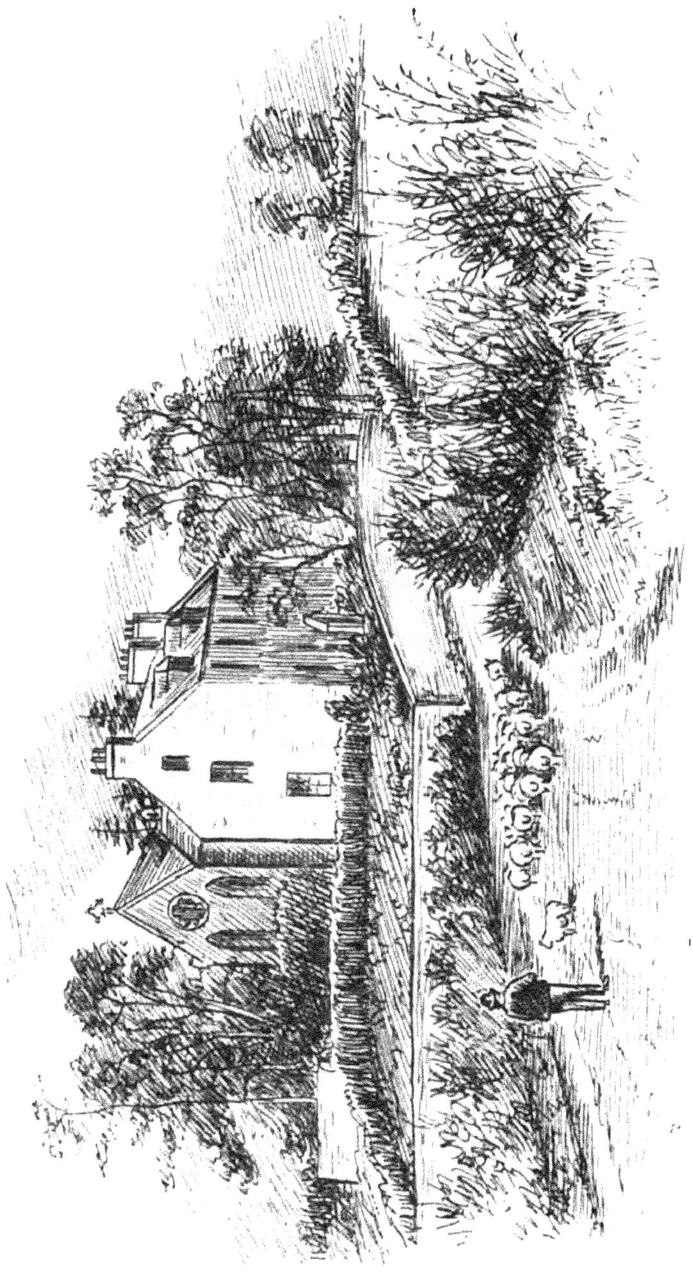

Sale of Right of Presentation.

desire of the remnant members of Council, have subscribed these presents, and the common seal of the said city is hereunto affixed. At Edinburgh the twenty-seventh day of February one thousand seven hundred and sixty years, before these witnesses, George Lindsay, Deputy Town Clerk of Edinburgh ; Hugh Buchan, writer there ; and the said John Forbes, subscribitur (1760); George Drummond, Provost; Da. Flint, B.; Adam Fairholm, B.; Gilb. Lawrie, B.; Rob. Selkrig, B.; John Carmichael, D. G.; Jas. Guthrie, Tr. Ita esse ut promititur ego Gulielmus Forbes. William Forbes.

" Hugh Buchan, *Witness*.

" John Forbes, ..

After the storm of 1843, the Town Council considered it advisable to sell the right of presentation to the parishes of Currie, Wemyss, and Fala, and they were consequently put up for public sale on Wednesday, the 14th January 1846.

The upset price was, Currie and Wemyss each £700, and Fala £250. They were withdrawn, as no offer was made. An attempt was again made in March of the same year to sell at the reduced price of £500 for Currie and Wemyss each, and £250 for Fala, but with a like success.

At this stage Mr Walter Cook, W.S., in name and by authority of the Principal and Professors of the University, lodged a protest against the proceeds of these sales being applied to any other purpose than that under which they are held. They urged that, by their charter of 4th April 1584, they had certain rights in these presentations, and that the price received should be invested for the use of the Principal and Professors, as they represent in their official capacity the educational interests of the burgh.

The claim was not admitted, and the University allowed it to drop. On the following August, the right of presentation to the parish of Currie was bought by Sir James Gibson-Craig, Bart., for £500. The alternate right to Fala and Soutra was bought by Mr George Grant, advocate, for £150, and the right of presentation to Wemyss parish was bought by Mr John Angus, Aberdeen, for £500.

Mr Grant, who bought the right of presentation to Fala and Soutra, never exercised it, but at Martinmas, 1860, he sold it to Mrs Ferguson Blair of Balthayock (now the Honourable Mrs Arbuthnot) for the sum of £460. When patronage was abolished, patrons were empowered to claim compensation, which was to be fixed by order of the Sheriff. Lord Stair generously gave up his claim and got nothing, but Mrs Arbuthnot claimed, and was afterwards paid the sum of £27, 6s. 6d.

CHAPTER X.

MINISTERS OF THE PARISH.

Thomas Cairns, the last Roman Catholic Vicar—The Rev. Messrs. Frank, Johnstoun, Henderson, Hastie, Carkettill, Carmichael, Thomsone, Porteous, Logan, Moodie, Johnstoune, Grant, Cavers, and Simpson—Battle of Prestonpans—The Rev. Messrs Wotherspoon, Gourlay, Sprott, Singers, Sherriff, Harkness, Munro, Ingram, Thomson, and Hunter.

FEW parishes in Scotland have preserved for them the name of the last parish priest who officiated during the time of the Reformation.

It appears that the property at Hawick which the Soutra Monastery possessed, and which was transferred to the Trinity College, Edinburgh, retained its name, "Soutra Croft," and was handed over again to Soutra in 1566. That year the "King and Queen" (Queen Mary and Darnley), two months before the murder of Rizzio at Holyrood, confirmed a charter giving to Dominus Thomas Cairns, the chaplain of the altar of the Blessed Virgin Mary of the subordinate church of Soutra, by the consent of Dominus George Clapperton, Provost of the Holy Trinity College Church of Edinburgh, the feudal land held by William Scott, in Hawick; a croft of land called Soutra Croft, an acre called Blackie's Acre, and a croft called Campiri Croft.

Thomas Cairns must have been officiating at this time; and as it was six years after the Reformation, and as the first Presbyterian minister was placed the next year, it is quite possible that the one left the same day the other came, or may even have officiated together in the same church at the same time. This was no uncommon practice, for the Roman priest to conduct services *à la* Roman in the morning, and the Presbyterian at noon.

1. William Frank is the first Presbyterian minister. He was ordained in 1567, lived in the manse at Soutra, and had under his charge Fala, Soutra, and Keith-Humbie, which is the southern part of the present parish of Humbie. He had also three readers under his charge, who officiated respectively in each of the parishes. Of their names only one survives, that of James Murray, whose salary was twenty-five merks a year. The income of the minister was £30 Scots for Soutra, nothing, as far as can be ascertained, for Fala, and the vicarage teinds for Keith-Humbie. He was also in possession of both the Fala and Soutra glebes.

2. In 1574, he was translated to Lauder, and was succeeded that same year by Adam Johnstoune. Under this minister Keith-Humbie was separated from Fala and Soutra, and Creichton was annexed in its place. He also had three readers under his charge, and lived at Soutra. The Soutra reader was paid twenty merks, and had also the kirk lands.

3. In 1589, Crichton was separated from Soutra and Fala, at which time Adam Johnstoune demitted office to give place to James Henderson, the first of the Episcopalian ministers under James VI. All that is recorded of him is that he left in a disorderly manner on 21st May 1590.

4. Early in 1591, James Hastie, M.A., was translated from Clerkington to Fala, where he resided. He got in the following year Soutra also under his charge. He continued

Rev. James Porteous, M.A.

minister to 1595, when he was appointed to the ministry of the parish of Temple. For him "the stipend was insufficient."

5. In 1596, Patrick Carkettill, M.A., a student of Edinburgh University, where he also laureated, was admitted to the ministry. He continued for two years, when he was translated to Stenton. In 1602 he was presented to the living of Humbie by King James VI., where he spent his days.

6. Patrick Carmichael, M.A., a distinguished student of Edinburgh University, under the regency of Mr Charles Fernie, was admitted minister of Fala and Soutra in 1599. He was translated to Aberdour, Fife, in 1602.

7. Thomas Thomsone, M.A., a graduate of St Andrews University, was appointed minister in 1605. He only remained five years, being translated to Hopkirk in 1609.

8. James Porteous, M.A., studied and graduated in 1598 at the University of St Andrews, was presented to the vicarage by James VI., and was translated to Lasswade in 1615. While minister of Lasswade, he was summoned by the High Commission, which met at Edinburgh, for not adopting the five articles of Perth. In 1617 the General Assembly met at Perth, after the King's return to England, to consider and sanction the late innovations in the constitution of the Church. After great opposition, the Assembly gave its sanction to five usages adopted by, and from, the Church of England :—1. That the Lord's Supper should be received kneeling. 2. That the Sacrament should be administered in private to the sick. 3. That baptism may be administered in private. 4. That children should receive confirmation when

they arrived at a proper age. 5. That the anniversaries of the Nativity, Passion, Resurrection, and Ascension of Christ, and Pentecost, should be observed as solemn days. Porteous died in 1643.

9. John Logan, M.A., studied at the University of Edinburgh, where he took his degree in 1611. He was licensed by the Edinburgh Presbytery, and recommended by them to the Town Council of Edinburgh, who presented him to the living in August 1616. This is the first appointment that is recorded by the Town Council made by them. Logan was the last of the ministers who lived at Soutra. He left in 1618, and took up his abode in Fala Manse, where the ministers have lived ever since. Before this the two parishes, although having only at times one minister, were looked upon as separate parishes, but this year they were united. In 1624 Soutra church was given up, Fala church was repaired, and has been used as the church for both parishes ever since. In 1627 there were one hundred and sixty communicants, as shown by the return to the Royal Commission by Charles I. on ecclesiastical affairs.

It is strange that Logan neither got into the "Bishop's drag-net" of 1663, nor demitted office when, by Act of Parliament, Presbyterianism was declared illegal, and the attendance on Episcopal worship made compulsory. Woodrow says that he, along with William Calderwood of Heriot, Adam Penman of Cockpen, and Gideon Penman of Crichton, all conformed; but that is not so, for, when an attempt was made to force him to conform in 1674, he demitted office. How he escaped these eleven years is an unsolved riddle.

10. George Moodie, M.A., a student of Edinburgh Uni-

Rev. Walter Cavers, M.A.

versity, laureated in 1669, and was licensed by the Bishop of Edinburgh in 1673. He was presented to the living of Fala as vicar by Thomas Hamilton of Preston in 1674. He continued Episcopal vicar up to 1681, when he was deprived of office by refusing to take the Test Act by Charles II., and swear for "King, Kirk, and Country."

11. He was succeeded by George Johnstoune, M.A., a student and graduate of Edinburgh University, in 1682. He was presented by the Town Council of Edinburgh, and ordained by the Bishops, 12th January 1683. He was translated to Burntisland in 1688.

12. Alexander Grant, M.A., son of Duncan Grant of Branchell, studied and graduated at the University and King's College, Aberdeen, in 1676. He was ordained by the Bishop of Edinburgh in 1688, and continued minister only for one year, as he would not read the proclamation of the estates, and also refused to pray for King William and Queen Mary. He was the last of the Episcopal ministers, and might have continued for many years, as far as the parishioners were concerned, if he had not been expelled by the Privy Council. It is worthy of note that the congregation retained the Episcopal attitude of worship up to a few years ago. They stood both at prayer and singing.

13. The parish remained vacant for eight years, until Walter Cavers, M.A., was appointed, the first of the unbroken chain of Presbyterian ministers. He was a graduate of Edinburgh University, which he left in 1692. He was called and ordained to the parish on the 21st September 1697. The congregation or parishioners had taken the presentation into their own hands, for the Edinburgh Town

Council records are silent about it. If the Town Council made the presentation, there was no record kept of it. Mr Cavers was minister of the parish for forty-five years, and died on the 3rd January 1742, aged seventy years. He, as far as can be traced from the kirk-session records, was a most exemplary minister, carefully guarding the discipline of the Church, faithfully preaching the Gospel, and dispensing the Sacraments. The records are better kept during his ministry than at any other period. Although the numbers cannot be given, the congregation must have been good, for he had the lairds of Fala, Soutra, Soutra Hill, Costerton, Whitburgh, Humbie, and Falahill Heriot, all members of the church. He, as is common to all good ministers, had a large family. There are ten children recorded as having been born in Fala Manse; and baptised in Fala Kirk. Their history cannot be traced.

14. The next to succeed Mr Cavers is Patrick Simpson, M.A., son of Mr Matthew Simpson, minister of Pencaitland. He studied at Edinburgh University, and graduated in 1733. He was licensed by the Presbytery of Haddington in July 1737, was presented to the living of Fala in June 1742 by Thomas Hamilton, Esq. of Fala, and was ordained in May 1743. This appointment must have been popular, for the collection on the day of his ordination was £6, 11s. 6d. (Scots). When it became known that Prince Charlie was raising an army to assert his claim to the crown of Scotland, the excitement it created caused the parishioners to prepare themselves for defence. The minister for some time drilled a small company at Fala village, and when it was known that the Prince and his army were on the east coast, Mr Simpson marched at the

FALA MANSE.

head of a small contingent to Prestonpans. When he arrived there, he got possession of a saddle-bag with six hundred guineas belonging to Sir John Cope's army, and was appointed to act as treasurer. After Cope's army was routed at the Battle of Prestonpans in 1745, they fled to Lauder by Fauside; but before the Fala minister left, he handed over the money to Dr Carlyle's father, who hid it for a time in the manse garden at Prestonpans. Mr Simpson's brother, Dr Colin Simpson, who distinguished himself by caring for the wounded and dying, after the battle carried the money to Bolton Manse, where it lay for a considerable time. The routing at Prestonpans was not looked upon in a very serious light by the Jacobites, however seriously the Whig army may have suffered. The various characters that appeared at the battle were made fun of by Adam Skirving, the farmer at Garleton, East Lothian, who wrote a rustic poem on the event. Mr Skirving was father to the late Mr Skirving, R.S.A., the distinguished artist, and grandfather to Mr Ainslie, the present proprietor of Costerton, who is in possession of portraits of the poet, the artist himself, and other members of this distinguished family. These portraits form a part of a most interesting collection of pictures and articles of vertu at Costerton House, one of the prettiest mansions in the district. There were several ministers at the battle along with Simpson. Mr Monteith, minister of Longformacus, was well-known for his distinguished horsemanship, and also well-known to Mr Skirving. Of him he writes—

"Monteith the great, where Hersell sate,
 Un'wares did ding her ower, man,

> Yet wadna stand to bear a hand,
> But aff fou fast did scour, man,
> O'er Soutra hill, ere he stood still,
> Before he tasted meat, man;
> Troth, he may brag of his swift nag
> That bare him aff sae fleet, man."

Mr Simpson being a keen soldier, and having little experience, made it his boast the day before the battle that he would convince the rebels of their error by the pistols he carried. He had for that purpose two in his pocket, two in his holsters, and one in his belt. It has been often conjectured if they were of Fala make.

> " And Simpson keen, to clear the een
>   Of rebels far in wrang, man,
> Did never strive, wi' pistols five,
>   But gallop'd wi' the thrang, man;
> He turned his back, and in a crack
>   Was cleanly out of sight, man,
> And thought it best; it was nae jest
>   Wi' Highlanders to fight, man."

After the battle, Mr Simpson resided for about three months at Berwick, afraid of coming to Fala, as he learned that the Prince and his army were coming by Fala to Carlisle. The minister returned to his parish at the beginning of the year, to be taken prisoner. He was removed to Stirling, where he lay for about three weeks, but was afterwards liberated. He always belonged to the advanced party in the Church; and when Jupiter Carlyle of Inveresk was libelled by the Presbytery of Dalkeith for attending the representation of the Tragedy of Douglas by Home, Simpson was one of his strong supporters, along with Logan, minister of Ormiston.

In 1759, he got a presentation to the parish of Clunie, which he accepted, and left Fala at the end of that year.

15. William Wotherspoon, licensed by the Presbytery of Dalkeith, on the 19th August 1757, presented by the Town Council of Edinburgh, and ordained to the parish on the 19th September 1760. From the frequency of the entry in the session records "No sermon," it may be assumed that Mr Wotherspoon was of delicate health. He died on the last day of May 1763, in the third year of his ministry.

16. John Gourlay, M.A., the next minister, a student and graduate of St Andrews University. He was licensed in 1763, presented to the parish of Fala by Thomas Hamilton M'Gill, Esq. of Fala, and ordained on the 11th May 1764. He, while minister, got the lead tokens made which were used up to the year 1880. After a ministry of nine years, he was translated to Crichton in 1773.

17. The next was William Sprott, who was presented by the Town Council of Edinburgh in September 1773, and ordained to the parish in April 1774. He, like the last whom the Town Council presented, was always in delicate health. He was a man who was greatly beloved by his people; for, when he wanted to resign in 1790, he was influenced by them to continue in office, which was not long, for in 1791 he died, deeply lamented by all who knew him.

18. The next minister, Archibald Singers, was born in the parish of Kinghorn, Fife, in July 1752, was educated at the parish school there, and at the University of Edinburgh. He was elected master of George Heriot's Hospital in 1776;

licensed by the Presbytery of Edinburgh on the 30th August 1780; presented to the parish of Fala by Lady Dalrymple Hamilton M'Gill, with consent of Sir John Dalrymple, Bart., the 1st November 1790; and ordained on the 20th April 1791. Mr Singers, like some of his predecessors, was a faithful minister of the Gospel, and liked by everybody, except a few of the village Dissenters, who tried to get him into trouble in 1815. A petition was presented to the Sheriff by a William Pearson and others against Mr Singers, for refusing to give a greater allowance of poor money to the petitioner. At a meeting of the heritors and kirk-session of Fala, it turned out that Pearson was not in need of more than he was getting, that he possessed money, and was spending it foolishly, and that the whole case was got up against the minister through ill-feeling. The heritors approved of Mr Singers' conduct, supported him in the bogus trial, and at last got the case quashed, and the costs thrown upon the complainers. This case created considerable feeling in the parish, but failed in its object—viz., to get a schism among the parishioners, with a view to increase the Dissenting congregation. Mr Singers wrote the article in Sinclair's Statistical Account of 1794 on Fala parish, which is characterised by a bitter attack on those whom he designates the "great ones" for their absence from the parish, and non-attendance on public worship, and also on account of the smallness of the stipend. He had reasons to complain of the latter, for he began a process of stipend augmentation before the Court of Teinds, and not only lost his case, but lost also about one-eighth part of his income, as the last augmentation, which was enjoyed for about a hundred years, was declared illegal. He says: "If we take into

Rev. Archibald Singers.

account the remarkable high price of provision here, this small sum (about £60 a year) is very inadequate to the maintenance of a family, unless they are clothed, like the Baptist of old, in coats of skins, and live, too, like him, upon locust and wild honey." Owing to his superior knowledge of ecclesiastical law, and his faithful attendance on the Church Courts, he was, when a vacancy occurred, appointed clerk to the Presbytery of Dalkeith, which office he held for nearly a quarter of a century. In everything he was thorough; the kirk-session and the Presbytery minutes bear this out. He was eloquent as a preacher, and his name lives still among the older parishioners.

When a member of the General Assembly at the beginning of this century, it was proposed to appoint a committee to revise the old Scottish Psalmody. One gentleman, amidst great laughter, proposed—

Archibald Singers of Fal-law;
Harry Sangster of Hum-bie;
David Pyper of Pencait-land; and
Robert Longrymer of Hadding-toun.

These gentlemen all happened to be the ministers of the respective parishes named at the same time.

Old age at last came upon Mr Singers; and in 1824 he was laid aside under paralysis, and became quite unfit for his ministerial duties. The parish became neglected, and in 1827 Sir John H. Dalrymple wrote to the Town Council of Edinburgh, asking them to appoint an assistant and successor, sending at the same time a petition signed by about 350 out of 400 parishioners, praying that Mr Sherriff, Mr Singers' assistant, be presented to the parish. The Town Council taking no notice of these communications, Sir John Dalrymple wrote again from Oxenfoord, under date the 13th November 1827, in which letter he says:—". . . I refer your Lordships . . . to the deplorable state in which the parish of Fala is at this moment. Mr Singers may live for years, but his mind is quite gone; so he cannot administer baptism, and children in the parish are now unbaptised. There is no church discipline, as there is no one to take cognisance of the conduct of the people, for there is not an elder in the parish. I might mention other things, but I feel convinced that I have said enough to draw your Lordships' immediate attention to a subject of such importance."

A committee of the Town Council was appointed to consider the matter, and afterwards it was agreed to appoint Mr Sherriff. Mr Singers removed from the manse early in 1828, and went to reside at Belhaven, where he died on the 8th October 1830, in the seventy-ninth year of his age, and in the fortieth of his ministry. He married Mary Lothian in December 1780, and had two children—Archibald, who became a banker at Newcastle; and Ann, who became the wife of the Rev. James Stirling, minister of Cockburnspath. Both Mr Singers and his wife were buried in Fala Churchyard.

19. Thomas Sherriff, who acted as assistant to Mr Singers for six years; by the strong desire of the heritors and parishioners, was presented to the parish by the Town Council of Edinburgh in January, and ordained assistant and successor on the 9th May 1828. He belonged to Tweedside, was educated at Edinburgh University, and licensed by the Presbytery of Chirnside in 1822. After a short ministry of eight years, he died in 1836, in the forty-sixth year of his

Rev. William Harkness.

age. Mr Sherriff, to the very last, was much liked by his people, being simple in his habits and evangelical in his preaching. He married Jessie M'Ewan while a student, and had several children—one, Arthur, who became a minister in New South Wales. Another son was a merchant in Edinburgh.

20. William Harkness, M.A., born at Mitchellstacks, in the parish of Morton, studied at the University of Edinburgh, and obtained his degree on the 30th March 1827. He was licensed by the Presbytery of Dumfries in 1833, and became tutor in the family of Sir James W. Moncrieff, Bart., until he was presented by the Commissioners for Sir John Hamilton Dalrymple, Bart., in 1836 to the parish. As the feeling was fast growing in the Church that the people should have the choice of their minister, the Commissioners gave a list of three names to the congregation, and assured them that whichever minister from the three was chosen by the congregation would be presented by the Commissioners. If this method had been adopted generally throughout Scotland, there would have been no Free Church. Mr Harkness proved himself a good minister, and, having some private means beyond the stipend, was enabled to live in comparative comfort. He was not void of humour; for, on one occasion shortly after his appointment to Fala, he met the Lord Provost of Edinburgh, who congratulated him on the appointment. Mr Harkness, in his reply, spoke of the living being very small, when the Lord Provost said, "that every minister should preach according to his stipend," meaning, of course, that ministers should not run into debt. Mr Harkness, taking the remark in its literal sense, said, "Preach according to his stipend! If I were to

preach according to my stipend, I would be a puir, puir han'." He was not destined to be minister long, for, on the 2nd July 1841, he died, in the fortieth year of his age, and in the fifth of his ministry. He married in September 1840, Anne, daughter of Hugh Rose, St Andrews.

21. Shortly after the decease of Mr Harkness, the congregation petitioned the Town Council of Edinburgh to present the Rev. David Brown, minister of Roslin, to the vacant church and parish. The heritors also petitioned on behalf of the said minister; but, when the Council met in October 1841 to elect a minister, it was resolved to rescind the motion to elect, and to allow the parishioners to elect from a leet, as had been done in the case of the previous minister. It was also moved to proceed with the election. Eighteen voted for the latter motion, and fourteen, including the Lord Provost and most of the bailies, voted for the former. The Lord Provost proposed the Rev. David Brown of Roslin, and Councillor Dunbar proposed Thomas Munro, M.A., of Edinburgh University, which motion was carried by a majority of two votes. When the Council again met to sign the presentation, the Council minute was objected to, and dissents were recorded. The presentation was sent to the Presbytery, who, at their first meeting, objected to it on the ground that Mr Munro was appointed to Fala *alone*, and not to Fala and Soutra. The Council agreed to prepare a new presentation, which was done at the expense of the presentee. When the matter again came before the Presbytery, the congregation and several members of Presbytery raised objections under Lord Aberdeen's Act, and an appeal was taken to Synod and General Assembly. The case was sent back by the Assembly

REV. JAMES HUNTER, F.S.A. SCOT.

Rev. James Ingram.

to the Presbytery; but, after a long and weary trial about technicalities, it again came to the Assembly, who at last instructed the Presbytery to proceed with the ordination, which took place on the 23rd June 1843. This exciting delay in the settlement of a minister did irreparable harm to the congregation, and to the cause of Christ in the parish, which has not got over it yet. Several of the best families left the congregation; and neither they nor those who have succeeded them ever enter a parish church. Under these trying circumstances, Mr Munro did his best, and proved himself an able minister of God's Word. In April 1844 he received a presentation to the parish of Campsie, which he accepted, and acted there as parish minister up to his death in 1879.

22. Mr Munro was succeeded by James Ingram, M.A., of Aberdeen University, a son of the Rev. William Ingram, minister of Echt, Aberdeenshire. After he was licensed in 1834, he was appointed and ordained to the Scotch Church, Amsterdam, where he laboured for nine years. He was presented to Fala in 1844 (in which year he wrote the new statistical account of this parish), by the Earl of Stair vice-patron. This appointment gave great satisfaction both to the congregation and the parish, as he, like some of those who had gone before, was a man of high thought and simple and sincere life. In 1858 he was presented to the living of Dumblane by the Crown; but the congregation, as in the case of his predecessor at Fala, raised all sorts of objections under Lord Aberdeen's Act. After his case dragged out a weary existence for three years, he was inducted to that parish in 1861. Through time he became exceedingly popular and much respected, outliving the opposition which he encountered

at first. He was minister of Dumblane for about eight years, where he died. While at Amsterdam, he married Maria Petronella De Boijs, the daughter of a well-to-do wood merchant, of an old Huguenot family. There were six children born to him at Fala Manse—Mary Ann and Johanna, who died and were buried at Dumblane; Helen, who died and was buried at Fala; William John, who became a wealthy banker at New York; Maria Petronella, who studied medicine at New York, and became a distinguished lady doctor in Brooklyn, and was thanked publicly a few years ago by the Mayor for her heroic conduct in sucking the mouth of a child who had diphtheria; and Jane, who married several years ago, James G. S. M'Kenzie, late merchant, Calcutta. Mrs M'Kenzie died two years ago at Eskbank, Dalkeith.

23. John Fernie Thomson, the son of a farmer in the parish of Tibbermuir, Perthshire, a distinguished classical student of St Andrews University, became classical master in Madras College, St Andrews, was licensed by the Presbytery of Perth, and ordained to the chapel at Howood, parish of Lochwinnoch, in 1857. After a year's service at Howood, he was translated to St Leonard's Chapel, Perth, where he laboured until he was appointed to Fala. In 1861 he was presented to the living of Fala by Mrs Ferguson Blair of Balthayock. He died in 1881, having completed a ministry of almost twenty years. He married, while at Perth, Jessie Wood Fisher, daughter of the Town Clerk of Cupar, Fife, who now resides with her family at Edinburgh.

24. The present minister, the first appointed under the Patronage Act of 1874, was ordained by the Presbytery of Dalkeith on the 24th January 1882.

Unbroken Succession of Ministers.

It is a question if any parish history in Scotland can show almost an unbroken chain of ministers, masters, and vicars back to 1160 A.D. like this parish.

From 1160 to 1462 there are recorded ten masters; from 1462 to 1567 four vicars, under the Roman Catholic regime; and from 1567 to 1891 there are recorded four Episcopal vicars and twenty Presbyterian ministers; many of whom were men of great ability, high character, and faithful in the discharge of their spiritual duties. Of all these there is not recorded a single scandal, or anything unworthy of their position and character. Of each it may be said—

> "He was a meek and holy man amid religious strife;
> And he, his pious rural flock, fed with the Bread of Life."

CHAPTER XI.

STIPEND OF FALA.

Stipend—Return to Ecclesiastical Commissioners in 1627—Down Grade—Uncertain Value—Unexhausted Teinds.

AS the stipend has all along played an important part in the existence of every minister, steps have always readily been taken both by the ministers and the Ecclesiastical Courts to ensure as far as possible a decent maintenance. As the Parliament allowed the Church to be unmercifully robbed at the Reformation, Knox and the other leaders in the Church enacted, in the first Book of Discipline, that the whole teinds go to provide an honest provision for ministers and their families, for the relief of the poor, and for the endowment of schools and universities. An Act was also passed the following year giving the whole of the thirds of all benefices to the ministers. If these laws had been carried out, the Church to-day would have been in a much healthier condition, and also in a much stronger position. But, as is well known, the greed of the barons was too much for the Church. Few, if any parish in Scotland, suffered so much as Fala and Soutra. There is only a mere fragment saved from what belonged to the minister. Step by step, by natural causes, and by flukes in law, the value of the stipend has gone down ever since the Reformation. Its history shows the depravity of human nature with a vengeance.

Fala Stipend.

> "Haste ye, haste ye, my fair Lady Joan,
> With this line to that saintly man.
> We'll give him dinner his heart to cheer,
> We've cheated him only threescore of bere."

As is recorded, the first Presbyterian minister had only £30 a year for Soutra, with glebe and manse, and also the glebe rent of Fala. What the real value of this £30 Scots would represent at the present time would be difficult to say. Arnot says, in his "History of Edinburgh," that a Scotch pound in the twelfth century contained about three times the quantity of our present pound, and thirty-six times more than our Scottish pound.

If the value of barley and oats be taken as a standard, and the price of barley and oats at the present compared with the price 700 years ago, it will be found that the purchasing power of a one-pound note sterling is, taking the average, twelve times of less value than the Scotch pound then. Taking also the price of barley and oats at the Reformation, and comparing that price with the present price, it will be found that the sterling pound can only purchase about one-eighth part of what the Scotch pound purchased then. The result is that the £30 a year enjoyed by the Rev. Mr Frank from the parish of Soutra, represented at the present time about £240 sterling a-year. Owing to the decrease of the purchasing power of money, and other causes, the ministers for sixty years after the Reformation suffered much throughout Scotland; and as an answer to their complaints, a Royal Commission was appointed in 1627 to inquire as to the ecclesiastical revenues of the Kirk. The Presbyteries were called upon to get from each minister a minute and authentic return of the existing parochial establishments within their bounds, of the state and amount of ecclesiastical property, and its application. Fortunately, the returns from the parish of Fala and Soutra are extant, and are here given.

"Sowtra and Fala Kirk.

"Att Dalkeith the tenth day of Maii, the yeir of God I^m VI^c twenty and seven yeiris.

"The quhilk day, Mr Johne Logane, minister at the Kirkis of Sowtra and Fala, togidder with Alexander Hodge Tailyeour and Adam Turnet, parocheneris nominat be the said minister as most judicious and indifferent, compeirit befoir the Moderator and Presbyterie of Dalkeith, and they gave all their aiths and wer admittet to the Tryall of the articles committed to them by the Lordis of His Majestie's Commission, and gave up their Declaration anent the saidis articles according to thair knawledge in manner following :—

The united Parishes of Sowtra and Fala.—"The Kirkis of Sowtra and Fala were united upon the twenty day of Februar 1618 yeiris. Before their union there was about four scoir of communicantis in each one of them, and now in them bothe being united together thair ar aucht scoir of communicantis.

"Both the Paroches lyeth contigue togidder, and ar bothe of a lyke lenth and breidth of the boundis of thrie myles in lenth and twa myles in breidth, bothe togidder. The farrest hous in the paroche fra the Kirk quhairto it belongis is two myllis.

"The Kirk of Sowtra was ane Abbey Kirk of old, quhilk Abbacy was first a benefice be itself, as We ar informed, and

Report to Royal Commissioners. 103

thereafter united with the provestrie of the Trinitie College in Edinburgh, as yet undissolved thairfra.

"The Kirk of Fala is ane Kirk of the Hospitall of Ednem, the benefice quhairto it belongis is the preceptorie of the said Hospitall. The patron of the Kirk of Sowtra is the town of Edinburgh, as is alledged by them. The patron of the Kirk of Fala is the Laird of Edmestoun of that ilk, quho is also patrone of the said preceptorie.

"The present stipend of the minister serveing the cure at the saidis Kirkis is twa hundreth and fyftie merkis, payit be the town of Edinburgh as titulars of the benefice and fetteris of the teyndis of the paroche, augmented be the last plat ten merkis; for befoir they payed bot twa hundreth and fourty merkis out of the personage and viccarage teyndis of Sowtra: and for the Kirk of Fala the minister's stipend presently is ane hundreth merkis payed be the Laird of Edmondstoun as tutour and administratour to his brother James Edmondstoun, out of the personage teyndis of the said paroche of Fala, and the viccarage teyndis of the paroche of Fala, quhilk, togidder with the viccarage of Ednem-Spittell (quhilk lay evermair to the viccarage of Fala as a pairt thairof), is estimat worthe fyftie pundis and 7 merk *communibus annis*, but without the viccarage of Ednem-Spittell is worthe fourtie pundis allenarly.

"Before the union, the minister's stipend was, for the Kirk of Fala allanerly the said viccarage, bot at the union the Laird of Edmonstoun was ordained to pay ane hundreth merkis more out of the personage teyndis of Fala.

"Now the hail stipend of the minister presently for his service at bothe Kirkis is four hundreth twenty-sax merkis, with the vicarage of Ednem-Spittell, or four hundreth and ten merkis without it.

"By and attour his two mansis and gleibs at the two Kirkis, quhilk, being valued, ar bothe worthe thretty-sax pundis yearly, and tene pundis ilk ane of them at the maist.

"There is, as We ar informed, a foundatioune for four heidman in Fala, bot quhat is become of the founded rent, and to quhom it is payed, We knaw not, although we have used all diligence we can to try the samyn. As for any other provision of any founded rent, ather for the poore or for a schoole in ony of the foirsaidis paroches, we knaw nane, althogh they ar bothe very necessary. As for prebendaries, chaplanaries, or frier landis, We knaw nane within the saidis paroches."

THE VALUATION OF THE ROWMES WITH THE PARISH OF SOWTRA.

"The saxtene husband landis of Sowtra barnis payis to William Borthwick, elder of Sowtra, thrie scoir and ellevin bollis of beir and nyne bollis ait meill and presentlie as the worthe of it *communibus annis*. And the pairtis and pendicles of the said rowme of Sowtra barnis, called Reid hall and Sowtra hill, payis thrie hundreth merkis, bot befoir all the said rowme with the pendicles foirsaidis payed thrie hundreth merkis. Bot were not the said rowme of Sowtra barnis hes the commodite of lyme quarrell, it was les worthy.

"The personage teyndis of the said rowme with the pendicles thairof (sa meikle as is led be the said William Borthwick) is worthe ane chalder of beir and twenty bollis of aitis presently; bot *communibus annis* it is worthe thretty bollis half beir half aite allanerly.

"The viccarage teyndis of Sowtra barnis is estimat worthe aucht pundis. The viccarage teyndis of Reidhall and Sowtra hill, quhilk ar the pendicles of Sowtra barnis ar estimat worthe twenty merkis *communibus annis*. There is, moreover, ane croft of land in Sowtra barnis quhairof the corne teynd is led out of the paroche be the gudman of Humby about aucht aikeris of land called Killcroft, with aucht riggis of ane uther croft nixt adjacent to it quhairof the teynd is estimat worthe twa bollis half beir half aitis.

"Bewest the Kirk of Sowtra lyeth thrie steidis called Gilstoun, Over Brotherstones and Nether Brotherstones, the farrest quhairof is tua miles fra the Kirk of Sowtra, quhille thrie rowmes ar of a lyke quantitie and qualetie, and ilk ane of the saidis thrie rowmes is worthe tua hundreth merkis of yeirly dewtie *communibus annis*, and worthe thrie bollis half beir half aitis for the personage teyndis, and worthe tuenty merkis for the viccarage teyndis, ilk ane of them *communibus annis*."

THE VALUATION OF THE ROWMES THAT LYETH WITHIN THE PAROCHE OF FALA.

"The landis of Falahall payis to the Laird of Edmonstoun as tutour foirsaid five hundreth merkis, but, *communibus annis*, it is worthe thrie hundreth and thrie scoir of merkis allanerly for stok and personage teyndis togidder, quhille threttie-sevin pundis *communibus annis*. The viccarage teyndis thairof ar estimat worthe aucht pundis.

"The landis of Fala payis to the Laird of Edmonstoune as tutour foirsaid ane thousand four scoir merkis for stock and personage teyndis togidder, quhille personage teyndis, being considderit severallie fra the stock, is estimat worthe ane hundreth and ellevin pundis, and the viccarage teyndis thairof worthe fyftene pundis *communibus annis*. The quhilk rowme of Fala his the commodetie of lyme quarrelle in the ground thairof, without the quhilk it wald not be so meikle worthe. And in respect it is ane late rowme, we think it payis tua hundredth merks abond the worthe of it in maill *communibus annis*.

"The mylne land of Fala is worthe thrie bollis of beir in stock and four pundis in teyndis, and tua merk and ane half for viccarage teynd.

"The landis of Broderscheill, being bot a gerse rowme subject to rotting in wet yeiris, presentlie payis fyve hundreth merkis, bot, *communibus annis*, it is worthe thrie hundreth and fyftie merkis in stock allanerly. It has little corne land quhairof the teynd corne is worthe twenty merkis, and the viccarage teyndis thereof saxtene pundis, *communibus annis*."

The above deposition shows that the stipend from the parish of Soutra should be 500 merks, and from Fala 100 merks, or £50, 7s. By the Act of Parliament of 1707, thirteen shillings and four pence represented one merk; and, accordingly, from the two parishes the stipend would be £212, 7s., even granting that the pound sterling has the same purchasing power that it had when this Act was passed.

As the result of the Royal Commission of 1627, an Act was passed in 1631. By this Act every proprietor was entitled to have his teinds valued, and either bought by him, or he paying the fifth part of the constant rent of stock and teind. The heritors of the parish took advantage of this Act, and got all their teinds valued, which valuation was considered to be fixed for all time coming. The following was allowed: —Twenty bolls and three firlots beir, twenty-four bolls of oats, and £437 Scots; which was a fair stipend for the time, and which would at the present be equal to the purchasing power of about £230. The lands of the parish of Fala, under stock and teinds, parsonage and viccarage, were valued at 1100 merks, and from that part of Fala parish called Brothershiels £300 Scots, which gives a total value of £86, 2s. $2\frac{8}{12}$d., according to the legal manner of computation. Under the Act, the fifth part being paid to the minister, which represents £17, 4s. $5\frac{1}{2}$d.

The stipend remained undisturbed until the minister, in the year 1727, raised a process of augmentation, modification, and locality. There was no augmentation given from the land of the parish of Soutra, but the stipend from the lands of Fala, Fala Hall, Fala Mill, Brothershiels was increased to £351, 13s. 4d. Scots, or £29, 6s. $4\frac{1}{4}$d. sterling. The minister continued to enjoy this increased stipend up to 1802, when a process again was raised to augment the stipend. The Lord Ordinary not only refused to grant an increase, but he held that the augmentation which was granted in 1727 was unlawful, as it represented more than one-fifth of the value of 1631. The stipend was then reduced from the lands of Fala to £17, 4s. $5\frac{1}{2}$d., although the rental is now thirteen times greater than it was when this stipend was fixed. This is the wrong, not only fixing the value of the pound Scots at the twelfth part of the pound sterling, but also fixing a value absolutely, without the slightest consideration for prospective change. Fala Parish, with an annual rental of £86, 2s. $2\frac{8}{12}$d, paid as much stipend in 1631 as it does at the present with an annual rental of about £1600. Fala parish, as far as paying stipend is concerned, is without a parallel in the whole of Scotland.

Of this unfortunate state of things the Parliament, not the heritors, came in 1825 to the rescue, by making up the legal stipend to £150 from the Exchequer. There is also an allowance of £8, 6s. 8d. for communion elements; and the right to pasture twenty sheep on Fala Moor, which was discovered some forty years ago, and which now is commuted into the equivalent of eight quarters of the best Mid-Lothian oats. There are also, of course, the two glebes and manse. The heritors have not as yet been called upon to erect a second manse, as it is generally recognised that one minister requires only one residence. The origin and history of the teinds of these two parishes show that the common idea and common practice that teinds are strictly parochial are entirely wrong. Before the Reformation teinds were inter-parochial and even after the Reformation teinds were constantly transferred from one parish to another. The teinds, for example, of Soutra Croft in this parish, were taken to the parish of Humbie. This was common all over Scotland. But an idea arose, not based upon an Act of Parliament, that teinds should be confined to the parish. This became a custom, and afterwards got incorporated into Acts of Parliament relating to teinds. This custom is much to be regretted, for if teinds were considered inter-parochial, as their origin and free use were for many years, certain anomalies which exist could be cured without having to seek for redress from Parliament. There are parishes where the free teind represents something like £1000 and £800 a year in each case, and which is being presently enjoyed by the heritors, who have no right to it. Should these teinds be "free" in the true sense of the term, and at the disposal of the Teind Court or other authority, the small livings of the Church would soon cease to exist, and a large surplus could be used for education, or any other philanthropic purpose.

It will be a matter of regret if the people of Scotland should ever lose sight of the unexhausted teinds, which might even yet prove a great blessing to many a poor minister, and bring cheer and comfort to many a straitened home.

CHAPTER XII.

RECORDS OF KIRK-SESSION.

Kirk-Session Records—Volumes I., II., III., IV., V.—Quaint Extracts—Register of Baptisms—Register of Proclamations—Register of Burials.

THE kirk-session records, both as to state of preservation, and to events and number of year which they record, will stand favourable comparison with many parishes in Scotland. They are in five volumes, the first bound in cloth of a modern date, and the others in calf bindings. Volume I. contains the session minutes and church-door collections from 1674 to 1723, with a blank from 1688 to 1713. All narrated from the 19th June 1715 has been copied and is found in the second volume. During the Episcopal period, the penmanship and ink used are superior to that which follows, showing that the Episcopalians took great care in recording the life and work of the Church. Many of the leaves are much torn, and much of the matter is unreadable.

Volume II. contains the session minutes and church-door collections from the 19th June 1715 to 24th May 1776, and is almost complete, except a blank here and there from 1740 to 1749. This volume is in a good state of preservation. It is bound in calf, and tied with leather thongs.

Volume III. contains the session minutes, with the names of the heads of families, and the record of other parochial matters from May 1776 to 1839. It is in splendid condition, and shows that the greatest care has been taken to give a full and perfect account of the kirk-session's transactions, and to write them out in the most perfect manner. The work almost throughout the whole book reflects the greatest credit on ministers and session-clerks.

Volume IV. gives the minutes of session from August 1839 to May 1874, and is in perfect condition.

Volume V. is the record from June 1874 to the present time.

Many of the entries in the older books, when the kirk-sessions had to do with almost everything in the parish, are quaint, and worthy of a place here.

"1674 6th August.—John Liddell, late schoolmaster, Carrington, got 8s.

1677 4th November.—9s. given to James Mylne to put ane handell on ye bell.

1678 January.—8s. to ane poore man who had his house burnt and all that he had.

,, December.—6s. for casting ye snow out of ye Kirke.

,, May.—James Dobie was rebuked by ye session for speaking in ye presence of ye minister in a wicked fashion.

,, May.—John Finlison and his wife complained against Bessie Borthwick stealing a pocke of corn.

1686 August.—13s. 4d. were given to John Binny for tickets for our Kirke.

,, November 7th.—8s. collected, which was given to a poore distressed man recommended by ye bishop.

1715 July 25th.—Itm for nails to ye tente, . 01 10 00

,, ,, Itm to Thomas Lato for fetching ye elements, . 01 00 00

Fala and Soutra.

1717	2nd April.—Itm given to Robert Houden for mending Soutra bridge and ye Kirk furms,	01 15 00
1718	13th July.—Collected for the use of the Lutheranian Church,	14 00 00
1719	20th December.—Col.: for the use of French Refuges settled in Saxony,	11 13 00
1720	30th October.—Imp.: given out to poor stranger being great object,	00 18 00
1722	March 8th.—Given by Jean Menteith, her penalty for ye sin of fornication with James Bowhill,	01 16 00
1721	Dec. 24th.—Imp.: bought from Robert Foular, tenant at Blackhouse, tua trees to be a bridge over Soutray Water, fur ye scholars' use at 15 sh. (Scots) ye price is	01 10 00
1722	Given out to Helen Riddell to pay for dying a goun and tailors' wages,	00 10 06
1723	February 13th.—Itm given out to by four elns and ane half of black sairge to bind ye large moar cloth att sixteen shill. and six pennies Scots; ye elu is	03 14 04
,,	March 28th.—Imp. given out for the use of families in Newbottle by the accident of fire,	04 04 00
1727	April 2nd.—Collected for ye Bridge o' Dee,	06 08 09
1737	September 25th.—Itm. to John Houden for mending ye bridge at ye Kirke door,	00 15 10

David Maitland of Soutra.

1737	September 25th. Itm. ye same time for a bell towe, . . .	00 08 00
1742	March 13th.—To William Borthwick to hire a horse and other charges for himself when att Edinburgh about ye business of ye poore money, . .	01 10 00
1761	July 19th.—Coll.: one pound fourteen shillings sixpence Scots; eighteen shillings whereof was imposed as a fine by the Lieutenant upon twelve of his soldiers for not attending Church,	01 19 06

1715 Jully 23rd.—The Qlk day intimation was given that Sermon was to begin one Sabbath day att nine of the clock in the morning.

1717 February 25th.—After prayer sed: ye minister and elders, this day ye minister read a letter before ye session: it came from Mr Liver, min^r of the Gospel att Merton, concerning Janet Sympson, her bringing forth two children to the old Laird of Soutray. The session desired ye min^r to lay the affair before Soutray."

Janet appeared in due time, was rebuked by the minister before the congregation on three successive Sundays, and was absolved from the scandal; but David Maitland of Soutra refused again and again, which was reported to the kirk-session, and at last to the Presbytery. The Presbytery instructed him to come under Church discipline, which advice he took.

"1720 June 19th.—The Qlk day compeared David Maitland of Soutray before the Congregation for his sin of fornication w^t Janet Sympson, was called upon by the minister, seriously spoke to and sharply rebuked for his sin, exhorted to make public ackowledgement of his offence and declare his sense thereof w^t sorrow for ye same, he confessed his sin, promised repentance of and sorrow for yt and all oyr offences, absolved from ye scandall."

1724 June 14th.—This day being read by ye min^r from the pulpit threatnings of excommunication agt ye Laird of Crookstone and his servant Isobel Scot.

1748 January 2nd.—Itm to a pinte of whiskie to James Finlison's burriall . . 00 16 00
,, Itm for 4 dozen of pipes, 3 quarters of a pound of tobacco . . . 00 06 00
,, Itm the grave . . 00 13 06
,, Itm the bell . . 00 03 06"

The Parochial Registers of Baptisms, Marriages, and Burials for this Parish were transferred to the Register House, Edinburgh, when the Registration Act came into operation in 1855. The Register of Baptisms is from 1673 to 1819, but is awanting from 1689 to 1697, and Births are registered from 1819 to 1854, which makes almost a complete record. From 1855 to the present date the record has been carefully kept to satisfy the law of the Church. Here and there are to be found notices respecting the ministers, as ordinations, &c., and also the payments of the duty tax of threepence upon each baptism, which was levied for about twenty years at the close

Proclamation of Banns.

of last century. The entries are made after the custom of the times.

" 1673. Upon ye first day of May, ye Laird of Fala House had a bairn baptised John Hepburne.
1673. Upon ye 18 day of September, our min^r Mr George Moodie, had a child baptised, named Agnes. Witness, David Hepburne of Manderston, and James A——, late Provost of Edinburgh.
1679. Upon ye 29th day of April, Major William Borthwick of Johnstounburn, ane childe baptised, named Marion. Witness, &c.
1679. Upon ye 27th day of Maii, John Borthwick of Costerton, had a child baptised, named Helen. Witness —John Moir, laird of Falahill, and John Pringle of Soutrahill.
1722. November 18th.—Ye ilk day a poore stranger had a child baptised, named Walter. Witness—Thomas Houden and Thomas Grinlay.
1774. July 16th—A child found at the gate of Fala House, was baptised, named William Fala.
1791. July 20th.—The which day Alexander Falconer, Esq. of Woodcote Park, and Mrs Matilda Clark, his spouse, had a son born and baptised by the Rev. Mr Simpson, one of the ministers, Edinburgh, named George Hemel."

The Register of Proclamations and of Marriages is complete from 1675 to 1847, except for the eleven years from 1686 to 1697. They have been carefully recorded, and the fee of

5s. always paid, except in those cases which were exempt by order of the kirk-session. Those who were irregularly married had to appear before the minister for rebuke, after which the marriage was registered. The following is a specimen :—

"1750. June 15th.—The which day William Home and Marion Carter was called before the minister in the manse, and in presence of Thomas Borthwick and William Hoy, they compeiring, were questioned anent a report of their irregular marriage. They owned they were married at Edinburgh Oct. last, and produced marriage lines bearing date the 15th of the said month, and had lived as man and wife ever since. The minister declared them married persons, and sharply rebuked them for their breach of order of the Church, and their contempt of that as well as of the civil law, and seriously exhorted them on all the duties incumbent upon them as man and wife, and to live and behave themselves as such in time to come, which they promised, and submittingly received tokens from the minister in order to partake of the Sacrament."

The Register of Burials has been ill kept, and only shows the names of those who were buried between 1829 and 1852. Subsequent to the last date, the Registrar only registers those who have died in the parish, and not those who are buried in Fala Churchyard. The result is that there is no account of the number of burials that took place, which is a matter of reproach and regret.

CHAPTER XIII.

BOARDS OF THE PARISH.

Parochial Board—School Board—Schoolmasters—Libraries—Charities—Friendly Society.

THE adoption of the Poor Law Act of 1845 brought relief to the kirk-session of the parish, as there was great difficulty in raising as much money as would supply the wants of the deserving poor. This arose very much owing to the non-residence of the heritors, and from the general condition of the parishioners. The church-door collections proved inadequate, and every year the minister and kirk-session made appeals to friends and others outside the parish to make up any deficit. In 1846 the whole machinery of the Parochial Board, as required by law, was put into operation, which has continued up to the present time, and by which not only casual relief is given, but the aged and infirm are supported on a small allowance of from two shillings and sixpence to three shillings and sixpence per week. Fortunately for the ratepayers the number of paupers is small, and may soon disappear altogether if proper supervision is used, as the people are generally provident in their habits.

Continuously from the Reformation up to 1873, when the Scottish Education Act of 1872 came into force, a school was upheld in the parish, and was under the regime of the minister, kirk session, and heritors. The school at Soutra continued until the decay of the village, after which for a time the schoolmaster taught one month at the Fala school, and the next at the Soutra school. This went on for about fifty years, until the Soutra population got so small that the turn-out of children rendered it necessary to close altogether. What became of the Soutra school buildings nothing is known; they have left no record or mark behind. After the rise of the Secession Church, the parents belonging to that "body" expressed a wish that their children should be taught "*à la* Secession." A teacher was employed, an opposition school was opened, and a great halo of romance and interest was thrown around the enterprise, which made it up to 1860 a success. The neglect of the parish school buildings also tended to drive the children to another school.

The education of the parish was at a low ebb in 1873, when the present school system began. The school was getting out of repair, and no attempt was made to supply those helps and means which modern education demands. The teacher, Mr Whiteford, one of the most respected of men, having all the *esprit de corps* of the old parochial schoolmaster which has made Scotland great, was becoming unable, owing to old age, to perform his duty. No help was offered, and a pension refused. To employ a young man meant an increase of attendance at school, which the building could not accommodate, and a new and suitable building was out of the question. This state of affairs was continued year after year in anticipation of new laws. The Act of 1872 came as a great boon to the parishioners, and a great pecuniary relief to the heritors; for by this Act the burden of providing education for the parish was removed from them, as heritors, and placed upon the ratepayers. The Act was generous, as it did not recognise the right of compensation from those who were exempt from obligations, which had continued for about 350 years. This was not all in Fala parish. At the second meeting of the new School Board, which was held on the 18th October 1873, it was resolved to erect a new school and master's house on a new site, at a cost of about £1000. This was carried out. A loan was got from the Educational Commissioners of £800, the payment of which was to be spread over a period of forty-five years. A grant in aid was also got of £168, 13s. 9d., and the old school, school-house, and garden were sold to Lord Stair for the sum of £113, 9s. 0d. The schoolmaster's house was very soon found to be inadequate, and in 1886 an addition was made at a further cost of £150.

Out of all this the parish minister was kept. The first Board, which was appointed by the Board of Education, consisted of Lord Stair's local factor, three of his tenants, and another person.

When the second election came round in 1876, a report was circulated that the same Board must be returned, otherwise the Government would not finish the promised grant, as the school buildings were not complete, which would bring the ratepayers into great pecuniary difficulties. This game was successful among a simple people, and the ministers were again left out. After it was too late, a reaction set in, and the ministers and others were enabled to keep out both factor and tenants on the occasion of the election to the third Board. "Use and wont" was resolved upon, and ever since the Board has done its work in peace and goodwill. The school-rate for the parish is high. The school buildings show that the work and material generally are very inferior.

The schoolmasters have all along played an honourable and important part in the history of the parish, and seldom getting that recognition and reward which their work demands. Along with the position of teacher, they up till recent years acted also as reader or precentor, and in more modern times filled the office of inspector of poor, collector of parish rates, &c. They have always filled the office of session-clerk. In the early records appear the names of John Crichton, James Ronald, and John Knox; Crichton acting from 1673 till about 1696 at a salary of £18 Scots. Ronald was schoolmaster for a few years, and was succeeded by John Knox in 1710, at a salary of £30 Scots for teaching, £3, 8s. for acting as reader, £7 for precenting, and £3 for filling the office of session-clerk. In 1728, it was discovered that he had misappropriated the session funds, and after a lengthy trial and confession, he was found guilty and deposed. William Hogg was then appointed, at whose death James Finlison filled the office until his death in 1748. William Hoy was next, and he acted up to April 1774, when John Paterson was chosen. John Paterson continued in office till his death in 1817, and was succeeded by James Turnbull, who left in 1833 to fill a more remunerative sphere in Gladsmuir. Alexander Murray was appointed in 1833, and was translated to Cranstoun in 1843. He was succeeded by James Whiteford, who continued in office until his death in 1873. From the manner and care shown in writing the kirk-session minutes, the last four named above seem to have been men of considerable culture and ability, and qualified to fill

Fala Charities.

the office of parochial teacher in any parish in Scotland. And for all this, the remuneration from the office remained very much stationary for the last 150 years, which was the small sum of £2, 4s. 4d. sterling, with garden, house, fees, and emoluments from other employment. The present teacher, Mr James Duncan, the first under the new educational system, was appointed in 1873 to succeed Mr Whiteford.

> "He comes—the sovereign of the little state,
>   And keeps the accustomed footpath to a hair;
> Yea, steady, as if piloted by Fate!
> He wears a dignified and solemn air:
>   Though it is said he is at times a fool—
>   As all men are—he is a wise man in the school.
>
> As if by magic, into being start
>   His subjects loyal, and crowd round the door.
> Hark! from the desk his prayer from the heart;
>   Now hundred tongues resume their various lore.
>   Loud and more loud the little Babel rings;
>   Now shines the dominie among earth's noblest things."

The parish is fairly well supplied with reading for the people. A colporteur goes round the parish to supply any literature that may be required month after month; and there are also two libraries, one under the auspices of the United Presbyterian Church, consisting of a large collection of miscellaneous books, and another, by some cause which cannot be explained, has been allowed to cease circulating. It may therefore be concluded that the supply is greater than the demand.

Of charities beyond the scope of the Parochial Board, the parish is well supplied. These consist of three—first, what is known as the "Herkes Bequest," which came into existence in 1845, and which was transferred, by the order of the

Scotch Educational Commissioners, from the United Presbyterian kirk-session, under whose charge it had formerly been, to the School Board for the parish. Its origin is as follows:—Peter Herkes, a tailor in Fala, died and left £100, the proceeds to go to assist poor parents in Fala in the education of their children. After its reception by the kirk-session, it was resolved to erect with it two cottages, which were to be named "The Herkes Cottages," the rents of which were to pay for education. An appeal was made, and Lord Stair generously gave a ninety-nine years' feu, free of feu-duty, of a small piece of land in the village upon which to erect the cottages. The farmers and others, without distinction of religious sectarianism, all assisted in the good work, which soon became an accomplished fact.

Second, the United Presbyterian kirk-session has also in their hands a small endowment of about £5 a year for the poor in connection with their congregation, which was left by a man in Lauder, of the name of Shiels.

Third, in the year 1840 a Friendly Society for the parish was instituted, and which has existed ever since with comparative success. The rules were carefully drawn up by the parish minister, the late Mr John Paterson, and John Jones. Each member pays one shilling per month to the funds; and during sickness the allowance is five shillings per week, which amount decreases if the recipient remains for a long time unable to return to his employment. There is also as funeral money an allowance of £4 for a member or member's wife, and £1 for a child under twelve years of age. The society dissolves every year on the first Tuesday of January, and the surplus funds are equally divided among the members.

CHAPTER XIV.

FALA SECESSION CHURCH.

The Secession Church—Its Origin – Ministers—Sir William Johnston—Congregation—Anniversary.

THE Secession Congregation of Fala had its origin in 1779 by a few members living in the district, who were attending the Secession churches at Stow and Dalkeith, joining together, and petitioning their respective sessions to give them sermons at Fala. Both sessions refused the petitions; but the petitioners, by protest and appeal, carried their case to the Presbytery. As there was considerable opposition to this movement by the respective congregations concerned, the Presbytery agreed to transmit the petitions to the Synod. The Synod agreed to send one of their number, the Rev. William Kedstone of Stow, to preach for the first time, and to continue the supply, the record says, as often as their other calls would permit. After four years' casual sermon supply, the congregation took another step by petitioning the Presbytery to recognise the congregation as a distinct charge, and to settle among them a minister. This the Presbytery refused to do. Another protest and appeal was taken to the Synod, which, after hearing parties on both sides, agreed to allow the protest and appeal to lie on the table. At the next Synod in 1784, the question was again raised, and, after considerable deliberation, it was agreed by a majority of votes to sanction the charge. Three years afterwards a session was formed, consisting of the following persons—viz., James Johnstone, Roughmare; Robert Lees, farmer, Nether Brotherstones; George Rough, Pathhead; and the Rev. James M'Gilchrist as moderator *pro tem.* After the session was constituted, candidates were heard, and afterwards a leet was formed, Mr Thomas Aitchison and Mr James Blythe being nominated. The congregation, by a majority, elected Mr Blythe, and his ordination took place on the 12th November 1788. As there was no church, Mr Blythe was ordained in a tent erected in a small grass field to the north of Black Shiels Inn. Shortly afterwards, by the minister's exertion, the " Long Stable," an old building, the site of which is now occupied by the joiner's workshop, was cleaned out, and seated for a place of worship. The congregation grew and flourished, for after four years' existence it had a membership of about 300. Mr Blythe's ministry only lasted five years, for in 1793 he was deposed by the Synod, and emigrated to America. He got the first manse erected in 1791; and regarding it the session book has the following entry :—" The congregation having applied to the session for supplies of money from the daily collections to assist them in building the manse, the session agreed to lend them £10, free of interest." After Mr Blythe's deposition, the congregation went on hearing candidates for two years, after which Mr David Watson, Mr Archibald Harper, and Mr James Keith were nominated and voted upon. The majority of votes came out in favour of Mr Keith, and he was subsequently ordained on the 26th August 1795. It is strange that the session book is a blank during his ministry. His ordination is recorded, but that is all. Yet, from all that can be learned about him, he appears to have been the Christian gentleman. He was always on intimate terms with the parish minister. Having some private means, he farmed the parish glebe, kept a cow and pony, and lived in easy circumstances. At the beginning of his ministry he got the congregation to erect the present church, the "Meetin' House," by which name it is best known, which was finished in 1799; all the accounts being paid the same year Part of the work was done by contract and part by day's wages. The master joiner charged 1s. 9d. for his day's work, and his men were paid 1s. 8d. There is no account of Mr Keith's stipend. Although he was careful to record the birth and baptism of his children in the parochial registers, which lay in the hands of the parish minister, there is no record of his marriage. His sister was the mother of the late Sir William Johnston of Kirkhill, the founder of the well-known firm Messrs W. & A. K. Johnston, Geographers, Edinburgh. His father having died when William was a child, he and his mother went to reside at the U.P. Manse, Fala, where he was brought up. Often, after he came to prominence, he visited Fala, and spoke in glowing terms of the early days he spent there. He had a couplet which he often repeated, and which was inscribed by himself on the pane of glass in his bedroom window.

> "The midwife wheels us in,
> And death he wheels us out.
> Good gracious!
> How we're wheeled about."

The Rev. Mr Keith died on the 20th March 1833, in the sixtieth year of his age, and in the thirty-eighth year of his ministry. He was buried in Fala Churchyard, where a handsome monument stands to his memory.

The Rev. John Cooper, the successor to Mr Keith, was inducted to the church on the 2nd April, 1834. He had been a missionary for several years before at Hurnee, East Indies. Shortly after Mr Cooper's settlement, the congregation had reached the climax of its prosperity: the numbers of the congregation increased to about 400 communicants and a great number of adherents. He was popular. He became the farmer's minister. On the Sunday the people streamed to Fala "Meetin' House" from the south, from the north, from the east, and from the west. These were great days at Fala. From every farm within ten miles came pouring along every Sunday, farmer and grieve, herd and hind, with their wives and families, to hear Mr Cooper. As a preacher he was gifted. He could keep them entranced narrating his experiences in foreign lands for hours. When at rebuke before the congregation, he was severe,—a terror to evildoers. Some of his remarks on these high occasions cannot be reproduced. He was always spoken of as a warm preacher. On one occasion two hinds were making their way to church, one to the Meeting House, the other to the Parish Church. They began to discuss their respective ministers, and getting into a heat over the matter, the U.P. hind retorts by saying, "Man, he's a cauld, cauld minister, that o' yours." The answer was, "He may be cauld, but I'm shair yours is warm enouch, for he's aye smellin' o' brimstone." As old age came upon Mr Cooper, he began to go about to preach to children; and when he preached in Edinburgh and elsewhere, he could always get a crowded church. Being so much absent from

Rev. William Fraser.

his proper work, the Fala Congregation began to decline, and and in 1863 he resigned his pastorate, and went to live in Edinburgh.

His successor, the Rev. William Fraser, was ordained to the congregation on the 16th August 1864. During his ministry, owing to the depopulation which is so marked in the district, the congregation in numbers came down to a little over a hundred members. Yet, those who continued remained true and loyal to their Kirk and minister. Indeed, in this respect, they are a most exemplary and respectable congregation, which shows the power of voluntary invested interest. After a short illness brought on by cold, Mr Fraser died on Tuesday the 17th of February 1891, deeply mourned by his congregation and by all who knew him. By his exertions a new manse was erected in 1875, which cost over £1100, and which was raised and paid all in two or three years. On the hundredth anniversary of the founding of the congregation, which was celebrated on the 15th and 16th of July 1888, in reply to a gift of a purse of sovereigns and a silver salver, Mr Fraser said, "They had started on a new existence, 'owing no man anything;' they had more than left the ditch." This has been the congregation's principle, and this has been its success. They have practically realised what John Logan of Soutra teaches in the second of our Scottish Paraphrases, and which Mr Fraser was fond to quote—

> "O God of Bethel! by whose hand
> Thy people still are fed;
> Who through this weary pilgrimage
> Hast all our fathers led:

Fala and Soutra.

Our vows, our prayers, we now present
  Before Thy throne of grace :
God of our Fathers! be the God
  Of their succeeding race.

Through each perplexing path of life
  Our wand'ring footsteps guide ;
Give us each day our daily bread,
  And raiment fit provide.
O spread Thy cov'ring wings around,
  Till all our wand'rings cease,
And at our Father's loved abode
  Our souls arrive in peace.

Such blessings from Thy gracious hand
  Our humble pray'rs implore ;
And Thou shalt be our chosen God,
  And portion evermore."

FALA "MEETIN' HOUSE."

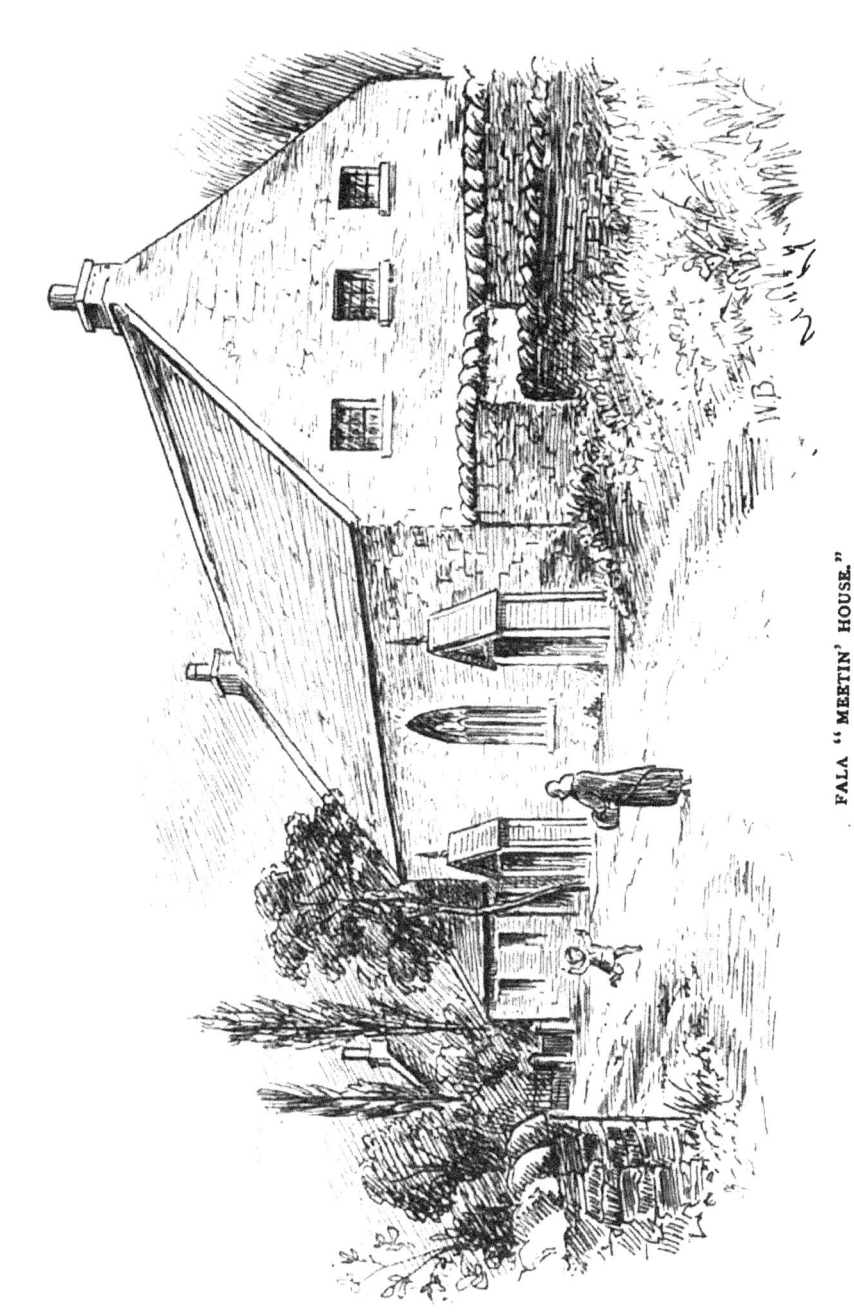

CHAPTER XV.

EMINENT MEN CONNECTED WITH THE PARISH.

Eminent Men—Andersons of Whitburgh—John Logan—Rev. William Anderson—Farm Tenants—Agriculture—Wages—General Condition of the People.

THE parish has not as yet produced many men who may be called great or eminent according to the usual standard. Yet, considering its isolated position and its paucity of inhabitants, there are a few connected with it who have left their mark on the history of the country. Reference has already been made to Lord Chancellor Eldon, Lord Wood, Lord Justice-General Inglis, Sir William Johnston, and Sir Thomas Napier.

The Andersons of Nether Brotherstones, whose residence was at Whitburgh, who have produced for four successive generations four distinguished generals, are worthily represented in the person of Major-General Anderson, C.B., a brave soldier of Indian Mutiny fame. His successful charge at Secundra Gunge, on the 5th January 1858, is recorded as among the most heroic deeds which have made our army greatly to be respected and feared by the enemy. This event forms the subject of a large and beautiful oil painting which now adorns the walls of the mess-room at Woolwich, and which was subscribed for in 1889 by officers connected with the Royal Horse Artillery. In this painting, General Anderson is the most prominent figure, and represents him in the act of charging the enemy.

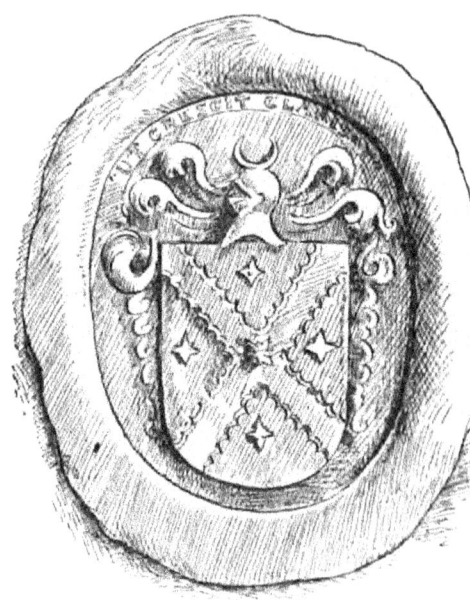

The Seal of the Andersons of Whitburgh.

John Logan, the author of "The Cuckoo," was born at Soutra Mains in 1748, his father, Robert Logan, being the tenant farmer there. He is usually described as belonging to the Secession Church at Fala, which did not exist till thirty-two years after his birth; and as there was no other Secession Church in the district, it may be affirmed with all safety that he and his parents belonged to the Parish Church. It so happens that owing to the death of James Finlison, the session-clerk, in 1748, and the frequent absence of the minister, the Rev. Patrick Simpson, there are several years of blanks in the session records. His brother's baptism is recorded, and his uncle's marriage and children's baptism are also recorded. The statement is given

Rev. John Logan.

by Dr M'Kelvie of Portmoak, who wrote Michael Bruce's life, and, as it is given on no authority, it may be concluded that Logan was no Dissenter. It is also narrated that his father removed with the family to Gosford, East Lothian, which does not agree with the fact that a Robert Logan, the same name as his father, was tenant in Soutra Mains for many years after 1748. Indeed, the Logans were tenants, and also members of the Parish Church, up to 1799. After receiving the rudiments of his education at the village school of Fala, he was sent to Musselburgh, where he was prepared for the university. At Edinburgh University he had as his companions Michael Bruce, the poet ; Mr

The Blair Seal.
(Presented to the Andersons of Whitburgh by "Prince Charlie").

Robertson, who became minister of Dalmeny, and author of the "Life of Queen Mary;" and others who spent their leisure in quoting and casting off poetical effusions. About this time Lord Elibank was attracted by his appearance and ability, and paid some attention to him, and also secured for him the appointment as tutor to John Sinclair, who afterwards became Sir John Sinclair, the author of the Statistical Account of Parishes in Scotland. In 1767, Michael Bruce died, and, by the request of some friends, Logan published three years after a volume of his poems, inserting some of his own, and among the latter was the "Ode to the Cuckoo," about the authorship of which considerable controversy has arisen. The last time this matter was publicly discussed was in a series of articles which appeared in *Good Words* about fifteen years ago, by the late Principal Shairp of St Andrews. He claimed Bruce as the author; but the late Dr Small, Librarian to the University of Edinburgh, reviewed all the arguments of the case, especially those raised by Principal Shairp, in an article which appeared in the *British and Foreign Evangelical Review* for July 1877, which afterwards was reprinted in pamphlet form. He concluded that there was no absolute proof that Logan was the author, but the evidence strongly supported that contention. Sir Walter Scott and the late Dr Laing were both in favour of Logan's authorship.

In 1773 Logan was licensed by the Presbytery of Edinburgh, and the same year was appointed minister of South Leith, in succession to the Rev. Dr Hunter. As minister, he had a short and brilliant career. In 1779 he lectured on philosophical subjects in St Mary's Church, Edinburgh, which attracted the attention of the *élite;* and night after night the place was crowded to excess. In the same year he also published several contributions "On the Manners and Government of Asia," which also attracted attention. His play called "Runnimede," which was issued in 1783, was named after the field in which King John and his barons met on the river Thames, between Staines and Windsor, and deals with the granting of the "Great.Charter" which secured for the nobles, clergy, and people of England a basis for the rights and liberties which they still enjoy. "Runnimede" was acted for a time in Covent Garden Theatre; but was latterly suppressed by order of the Chamberlain, as it was considered a breach of privilege against the House of Commons, and also because it might arouse public feeling in regard to the American War of Independence.

Logan, having fallen into intemperate habits, resigned his ministry in 1786, and the year afterwards went to London, where he led an unfortunate life, and died on the 28th of December 1788. After his death, two volumes of his sermons were published, which show that he was a man of considerable intellectual power, and of spiritual discernment. His life shows that man is a complex problem, a mass of contradictions, which gives to all this important lesson, "Never put your trust even in intellectual princes."

When the Paraphrases were adopted by the General Assembly of the Church of Scotland, eleven of Logan's productions were incorporated. He wrote Paraphrases 8, 9, 10, 11, 18, 31, 38, 48, 53, 58, and the last hymn at the end of the Paraphrases, which begins with the words, " The hour of my departure's come ; I hear the voice that calls me home,"

&c. About the 58th Paraphrase some controversy has arisen, and the friends of Bruce naturally claim it as his. It would appear that, as Bruce's life was honourable and his death natural, and as his friends were first in the field, they claimed everything that was of merit which was published under the joint authorship of Logan and Bruce. On the other hand, as Logan's life was unfortunate and his death untimely, he got little credit for what he had so successfully accomplished. But the time will come when his mistakes will be forgotten, and when he will be judged by the labours of his hands. Yes, his "Ode to the Cuckoo" and his Paraphrases will live when his essays, lectures, and sermons will be no more. Generations unborn will yet sing with feeling and pathos, as our fathers before us—

> "Where high the heav'nly temple stands,
> The house of God not made with hands,
> A great High Priest our nature wears,
> The Guardian of mankind appears.
>
> He who for men their surety stood,
> And pour'd on earth His precious blood,
> Pursues in heaven His mighty plan,
> The Saviour and the friend of man."

The Rev. William Anderson, one of the missionary pioneers to Old Calabar under the auspices of the United Presbyterian Church, although not exactly born in the parish, was identified with it for a number of years. It was while attending to the cattle at Fala Mains farm in 1828 that he got his first religious impressions, and resolved to dedicate his life to the preaching of the Gospel. On Fala Moor, during the few years he was engaged there, he often gave expression to his religious feelings and enthusiasm by preaching to the "cows, sheep, whaups, and peewits." In 1833-34 he worked on the "great road" which was being made, and which passes through the parish. After he got sufficient Latin and Greek, he left for the university, and through time became qualified for the position of missionary. He was largely instrumental, under the hands of a Divine Father in Heaven, in bringing the natives of Old Calabar out of a condition of cannibalism, superstition, and darkness, into Christian light and truth, and civilisation. His work was successful, and the Lord crowned it. After thirty-five years of faithful service, he returned to this country; and the few times that he has preached here, among those who were his own "kith and kin," the church was crowded. He still retains his Fala fire and enthusiasm.

At the beginning of this century David Hunter, the tenant of Soutra Mains farm, had two sons who stood well in their classes at the University of Edinburgh, and both became ministers. One was for many years the respected minister of Heriot, and the other went to China as a missionary, where he was successful. After a number of years' mission work he came home to spend his days, and took up his residence in London, where he died several years ago.

The farm tenants of the parish of Fala and Soutra have all along been, as a rule, men of character, credit, and enterprise. Those in Soutra, who fell into lands reclaimed by the monks, were always able to hold their own with any of their neighbours. Those in Fala, who were fortunate enough to be under the agricultural influence of the Hamiltons of Fala, always farmed "high," and produced sheep, horses, and cattle which commanded the highest prices in the open market. Thomas Baillie held the farm of Soutra Mains for about fifty years. The Logans entered in 1740, and farmed it for over forty years. William Hunter, who had been tenant of Fala Mill, succeeded the Logans; and his son, David Hunter, acted as elder in the parish for about thirty-five years. The Hunters left Soutra for Fala Mains, and, after occupying it for nearly forty years, they removed to Oxenfoord Mains, which they farmed till 1883. In Soutra the Gibsons followed the Hunters; and Andrew, who was the last in the farm, was elder for the parish for many years. Mr M'Niven and his son were next, and they were succeeded by Mr Pate the present tenant. Gilston and Over Brotherstones have been farmed by the Johnstones, Hasties, Taits, Mr Cossar of Heriot Town, and the present proprietor, Mr Dun.

Brothershiels has had as tenants, the Houdens, the Taylors, and for over sixty years the Inglis, who have been long known for their excellent breed of sheep. Brothershiels is also the birthplace of three or four distinguished ministers and missionaries of the name of Inglis. Fala Mains was for long in the hands of the Houdens; Mr Peter Burton, who was the respected elder for thirty years; and Mr D. Broomfield. Mr Prentice is the present tenant. The Olivers, Taylors, the Andersons, Herdmans, succeeded each other in Fala Hall, and the present tenant is Mr James Burton, the son of Mr Burton of Fala Mains, and has been in possession for twenty-five years. Fala Parks, after the removal of the proprietors of Fala from the parish, were farmed by the Murrays and Herdmans. Blackshiels, including Fala Mill lands and Fala Parks, were farmed for nearly half a century by Mr David Broomfield of Blackshiels Inn. In the inn Mr Broomfield succeeded the Roughheads, who succeeded the Taylors, the first innkeepers, after the erection of the present building. The present tenant of the lands is Mr Robert Broomfield, who got the inn abolished in 1880. The shootings, generally, in the parish, are let to yearly tenants, who pay a large rent, as game is plentiful and well preserved. The Messrs Herdman, Edinburgh, have had the Fala shootings, the best in the district, for thirteen years; and they succeeded Mr Charles Jenner of Easter Duddingston, who held them for nearly twenty years, and who always resided in the parish for a few months every year, and became thereby one of the most popular of "shooting tenants."

Owing to the improved methods of agriculture adopted by the Hamiltons of Fala 150 years ago, the parish has ever remained in a high state of cultivation. The soil of the arable lands is good, the fields well drained and sheltered, and the result is, the crops year after year will compare favourably with even those in more favoured quarters. Yet with all this, owing to foreign competition and other causes, the rents have gone down for the last twelve years, when, it may be said, they reached the highest point. The rental of the parish at the present time is about £3200. In 1844 it was £3000; in 1794, £1100; in 1727, £400; and in 1627, £160 sterling.

The wages of servants have increased at a greater ratio than the rental, and at the present time present a problem that requires careful handling. The labour question is putting the farmer into a state of fear and trembling, and what the issue may be remains to be seen. Male servants employed on farms are getting from £36 to £40 a year, with gains, house, and garden. In 1844 they got from £9 to £11, and in 1794 from £6 to £9, with the same additions.

Female domestic servants now get from £15 to £18 a year; at the beginning of the century they had from £3 to £4; and in the middle of the century from £5 to £7. Day labourers now demand three shillings a day, and were only paid one shilling and twopence ninety years ago.

The parish being purely rural, there are no public works of any kind, and nothing for young men to do when they arrive at manhood, except to work in connection with farming. The result is, whenever the young grow up they go off, and leave generally their parents behind. Some time ago there was worked on the north side of the parish, along the bank of the Cakemuir Burn, a small seam of coal, but as the quality was bad, and the means of getting it difficult, it was abandoned. The result of all this is that the population has gone down for many years. What the population was prior to the middle of last century would be difficult to say; but it must have been greater than since, for the small farms have been abolished, the village of Soutra demolished, and decay and ruin have come to the village of Fala itself. In 1755 the population was 312; in 1790, 372; in 1801, 354; and in 1841, 393, which increase was caused by the great coach traffic before the railways were developed. In 1871 it stood at 312, and last census (1891) gave only 264.

The people, being isolated from the great centres of civilisation, do not give much attention to those social problems

The Ploughman's Education. 139

which are continually agitating larger communities. Their whole time is occupied with their labours, with their kirk, market, and general country talk. They are, as a rule, a shrewd, clever people, living respectable lives, paying their way, and providing for old age. Longevity is common in the parish, and it is seldom that anyone dies under three score and ten years. The nature of the occupation, absence of much care and worry, and the fine blend of mountain and sea air, give health and vigour and stature to the people.

The only excitement is during a Parliamentary election. Many of them have come under the charm and spell of Mr Gladstone. After the extension of the franchise to householders in 1885, there was great excitement. One farmer in the parish, who served on Mr Gladstone's Committee, got the great statesman's photograph, and also a portrait, which was hung upon the farmhouse walls. On one occasion a hind from East Lothian called on one of the hinds under this farmer, and, in conversation about the Franchise Bill, said, "Man, Tam, you'll surely get grand calves noo?" "What way that?" says Tam. "Because I hear that the maister has got a French bull fra' Mr Gledstane."

Although here and there may be found a ploughman whose education has been neglected, as a rule they are well educated. The shepherds, gardeners, and gamekeepers are highly intelligent men, and will hold their own with many who are higher in the social scale. The general literature that is circulated, easy access to the daily and weekly newspapers, all help not only to educate, but also to stimulate and cheer what would otherwise be a very monotonous life. Long may they be kept from the snares and temptations of our modern civilisation, for

> "Ill fares the land, to hastening ills a prey,
> Where wealth accumulates and men decay;
> Princes and lords may flourish, or may fade,
> A breath can make them, as a breath has made.
> But a bold peasantry, their country's pride,
> When once destroyed can never be supplied."

The Ploughman's Education. 139

which are continually agitating larger communities. Their whole time is occupied with their labours, with their kirk, market, and general country talk. They are, as a rule, a shrewd, clever people, living respectable lives, paying their way, and providing for old age. Longevity is common in the parish, and it is seldom that anyone dies under three score and ten years. The nature of the occupation, absence of much care and worry, and the fine blend of mountain and sea air, give health and vigour and stature to the people.

The only excitement is during a Parliamentary election. Many of them have come under the charm and spell of Mr Gladstone. After the extension of the franchise to householders in 1885, there was great excitement. One farmer in the parish, who served on Mr Gladstone's Committee, got the great statesman's photograph, and also a portrait, which was hung upon the farmhouse walls. On one occasion a hind from East Lothian called on one of the hinds under this farmer, and, in conversation about the Franchise Bill, said, "Man, Tam, you'll surely get grand calves noo?" "What way that?" says Tam. "Because I hear that the maister has got a French bull fra' Mr Gledstane."

Although here and there may be found a ploughman whose education has been neglected, as a rule they are well educated. The shepherds, gardeners, and gamekeepers are highly intelligent men, and will hold their own with many who are higher in the social scale. The general literature that is circulated, easy access to the daily and weekly newspapers, all help not only to educate, but also to stimulate and cheer what would otherwise be a very monotonous life. Long may they be kept from the snares and temptations of our modern civilisation, for

> "Ill fares the land, to hastening ills a prey,
> Where wealth accumulates and men decay;
> Princes and lords may flourish, or may fade,
> A breath can make them, as a breath has made.
> But a bold peasantry, their country's pride,
> When once destroyed can never be supplied."

CHAPTER XVI.

CHARACTER OF PARISH AND PEOPLE.

The Perfect Rural Character of the Parish—The General Condition of the People—What they Read—Their Intelligence—Their Religion—Their Inquisitiveness—Their Politeness—Conscription—Home Life—Change in Food—Their Work—The Land Question—A Solution—A Blessing.

THERE is no parish within the same radius of Edinburgh that presents such perfect rural surroundings and life as the parish of Fala and Soutra. It has its hill and dale, mountain and stream, moor and marsh, woods and glens, and fields, pasture and arable. It has its old historical buildings and its modern mansion, its bield farmhouses with the adjoining steading, showing in season the well-filled stack-yard, and well-filled cattle and sheep pens. There are no outstanding features of newness to be met. Everything looks seasoned with age and respectability. Visit it to-day, and again after a lapse of ten years, and you find everything the same. It ever retains the same steady-going character, in spite of the rapid march of time and men in the world around. Owing to the dryness of the atmosphere, the absence of all smoke and smells, or anything that is offensive to health, the fine healthy occupation, and the simple and frugal ways of Fala life, give not only a great longevity to its inhabitants, but show to the outside observer few indications of changing life. And yet, although the parish retains this perfect rural character, it is not beyond the pale of civilisation. It has its post office and telegraph station. It has its daily connection with Tynehead Station on the Waverley route by post gig. It *now* has its coach daily to Dalkeith in the morning, and the return coach each evening. Your letters are handed to you every morning by half-past eight o'clock, and even at that hour you may read your copy of the *Scotsman* fresh from Edinburgh, giving a *resumé* of the principal topics which have appeared in the *London Times* of that same date. These are all "modern adjuncts" to the usual means in country parishes of carrying news and gossip. And these "means" have their effect on the character and lives of the people. The casual visitor from Edinburgh is apt to think that the people are simple. But to say that they are simple does not mean that they are stupid. An elder from Free St George's Church, Edinburgh, on one occasion was being shown the church, churchyard, &c., by the worthy beadle. As he thought the beadle simple, he began to make fun of him about the smallness of the kirk and congregation.

He next asked how many services were held on Sunday? The answer was, "Only ane, Sir, how mony would ye hae?" "Oh! that is nothing," says the worthy elder, "we have three or four services every Lord's day in our church in Edinburgh." "What kirk is that?" asked the beadle. "Free St George's, Edinburgh," was the reply. The beadle was as smart as he, and closed the conversation by the pauky reply, "Wi' a' your services, Sir, ye're no sae near heaven as we are." Whether the Fala folks, according to the beadle, are nearer heaven in the physical or spiritual sense, or both, remains to be seen.

Within the last few years a decided improvement has taken place in the character of the people, and now they will compare favourably with any people similarly situated in Scotland. The fewness of those who have been called before the kirk-session of late is the best proof. In the parish there is neither a teetotaler nor drunkard, and swearing is dying a natural death. The question may be asked, Has religion declined? It has not. It may not show the same fanatical devotion, or exhibit itself by continually quoting Scripture; but for true, honest life, in all its intelligence and humility, things, as far as can be discerned, never were better. No doubt, from the minister's standpoint, everything is not what may be desired. Church attendance is not good, and of those who attend on public worship the greater proportion are males. This is easily explained. The women are required at home to look after the house, children, and cattle, and prepare dinner for those who have gone to church. To all who live at a distance, attendance at church occupies several hours. They leave home before ten o'clock in the morning, and don't return till after two or three o'clock in the afternoon. This means a long day. The "terms," fairs, harvest, and sheep-shearing time, all affect the church attendance. Yet amongst them are many who are truly religious, showing their religion in their life-work and conduct, and ever ready and willing to assist those in need who call upon them. It must also be said that they are a truthful people, and, although remote from Highland character, show many of the Highland traits. They are slow to answer any question asked; and when an answer comes, it reminds you of the modern method of answering political questions. To the stranger they present a dull external, but within there is a general intelligence equal to the occasion. They are well read on the current political and social questions. *The Weekly Scotsman*, *The Dundee Weekly Advertiser*, *The People's Friend*, and *Modern Society* are carefully read and circulated, and read again. There is nothing in these journals that escapes them. Their contents are inwardly digested and discussed by the people at their work and in their social gatherings. These, with an occasional daily *Scotsman* and *Scottish Leader*, are practically the intellectual pabulum of the people. Although they are a Bible-loving, they are not a Bible-reading, people. Here and there are to be found men who are "mighty in Scripture," but they are the exception, and not the rule. They are slow to speak of religion, looking entirely to the minister for the outward expression of religious truth.

They are keen, cunning, and inquisitive. In the genealogy of their neighbours they are perfect, and can narrate with open candour and clearness the virtues and failings of generations that are gone. Each knows his neighbour's private affairs better than he himself sometimes knows them. It has been often said, "There are no secrets in Fala." The late Mr Cooper told his people on one occasion, "that on the great day of judgment all secrets would be made known, but there will be none from Fala, as they are all known already."

Every movement of the visitor, as well as neighbour, is watched. If the minister passes, the one neighbour runs to the other to tell that the minister has gone by, and to ask, "Whar will he be gane the day."

Want of Discipline.

Like the rural Scotch generally, the people are deficient in those outward signs of respect and politeness which characterise the peasantry in England and on the Continent.

The English who visit the district frankly say the people here have no manners. These are sadly deficient; but this work should be undertaken by the School Boards. It is to be expected that the time is not far distant when district Boards will take the place of parish Boards, and when these larger Boards will employ within their bounds a drill instructor to give gymnastic exercise and drill to every boy at school. If politeness is required, so are drill and discipline. The lads and boys and men do not know how to walk and carry themselves, because they have been neglected in the training of early years. This is an important National question, not only for the good of the individual, but also for the welfare of the nation. Every young boy and every young man should be well drilled. The great expense incurred in keeping up our army, and the great scarcity of recruits, in spite of all the inducements that are offered, indicate that the time has about come when the best solution of the army question may be found to be *a mild form of conscription.* What a blessing a year's drill would be to the young men of Fala and other Scotch rural parishes. It would do more than teach them politeness. It would be a lasting good to them as individuals, as well as a blessing to the nation.

It has often been said,—To judge of a nation you must see the people in their homes, you must know their habits, and learn their characteristics. The home is the nursery of the nation, and the country is the nursery of the towns. Too little attention has been given in the past to the "home life" of our Scottish peasantry. Who is to do it? it may be asked. A great and noble work in other countries has been done by the priest or spiritual adviser of the people in the way of directing home life. This has been much overlooked in Scotland. But in Scotland the minister is not alone sufficient for the task. Other help is required. For the minister to interfere alone, he is apt to be met by the answer to mind his own work. The growing freedom from ecclesiastical control indicates this answer. If this work is ever successfully accomplished, it can only be by the joint effort of minister and master. The home life and home habits in the whole district around show the necessity of teaching the people Domestic Economy, and how to spend a winter's evening in some easy useful occupation.

The local exhibitions of industrial work have not come too soon, and will yet do a good work by encouraging men and women in their spare moments to engage their attention with useful work. Satan finds mischief for idle hands; but by proper directions and encouragement Satan may yet be nonplussed. The local industrial exhibitions, representing several parishes, which have been held at Upper Keith on two occasions, are doing much good, by supplying a long felt want, and are worthy of greater support.

In regard to food, the habits of the people have changed much of late. The growing habit or custom of paying the wages of the farm labourers all in money, instead of the more ancient, in that of "gains" and money, is likely to lead to unfortunate results.

Since this change has taken place, the confectioner and jelly merchant hawk the country districts with their wares, and tempt the wives to buy. The result is that tea and jelly have taken the place of porridge and sweet milk. There is an old saying—

> That's what makes a man,
> A piece in ilka han'
> And a bannock in his bosom.

If the modern custom to ignore porridge and milk continues, and the want only supplied by tea and bread with jelly, the result will be disastrous to the stamina and health of the people. The thriftless mother may rear a thriftless son and a thriftless daughter, and the thriftless family may soon become a thriftless nation.

To those who have little knowledge of farm work, it appears to them both dull and monotonous; but to those who are acquainted with the various duties that fall to the lot of the ploughman, the work shows not only variety, but interest as well. Every season has a duty peculiar to itself. Seed-time and harvest, summer and winter, each bring a succession of change in farm work. There is something new to do every day, and all this is enlivened by an occasional trip to the market with the master's grain or cattle, when a small allowance is given to each to assist in entertaining himself and friends. The work, except at harvest, is not arduous, and no occupation is more healthy. The hours of labour, on an average for the year, do not exceed ten hours a day. Sunday work is the most disagreeable, as the ploughmen strongly believe in that day as a day of rest. But so far as is possible, both masters and servants observe the Sunday alike. There is no need for a Sunday Observance Society in this parish, unless to prohibit those who come in summer from the neighbouring towns to visit their friends. Since tolls have been abolished, there is a growing tendency for everybody in small towns who can turn out anything in the shape or name of vehicle, to run to visit the country districts. On summer Sunday evenings there is quite a procession of nondescript vehicles down Soutrahill towards Dalkeith and Tranent. This is the only Sunday disturbance that exists in the parish.

If the agricultural labourers were let alone, little would be heard of the cry for small holdings and crofts. The ploughmen in the district understand the practical difficulties in the way of subdividing the land better than many of those who run hither and thither over the face of the earth crying for three acres and a cow. Not that there is no land grievance, but the grievance is not peculiar to the ploughman, but to all who share in country or rural life. The small farms are disappearing along with the population everywhere, and the large ones are getting larger. But what is this but a necessity of the times? The great laws of supply and demand must operate in agriculture as in everything else. The subdivision of farms would only lead to national disasters and ruin, simply because of the enormous amount required to raise buildings and steadings, and to provide the modern and improved machinery that are required to enable the farmer to compete with the foreign market. This is the secret of agricultural commerce. And the saving of this expenditure enables the farmer to pay rent and taxes, and to compete in open market.

But apart from this, there is a grievance, and that grievance arises from the fact that many in these days who possess land never think of the moral obligations that are due towards those who live upon it, and who gather the rent. Absenteeism, which was the curse in Ireland, is also a running sore in Scotland. The people now are being educated, and they are beginning to ask how this one and that one came to possess these lands, and why they pocket the rent and take no interest in the welfare of the inhabitants? Not that all landlords are alike. There are some in Mid-Lothian whose names are a household word, who are not only a credit to their class, but by the faithful discharge of moral obligations, they are a restraining influence upon many who would rise up to bring this question to the front of political warfare. Few parishes have suffered more by the absent landlord than this, and this absence creates a discontent and a desire for redress. If something were done in the following ways to put this question upon a satisfactory basis, natural laws should be left to do the rest. The law of entail and primogeniture should be abolished. Free sale and free registration of land should become the law, and the local taxation *doubled* upon all properties that are non-residential. These, by the help of God, would end the only real land grievances that exist at the present moment, and, these secured and adopted in time, might go a long way towards destroying the growing demands for greater and more extravagant reforms which might bring the country to revolution. May the Giver of all

Good raise up and inspire men to solve for ever this land question, and

> " Long may the hardy sons of rustic toil
>   Be blest with health, and peace, and sweet content!
> And oh! may Heaven their simple lives prevent
>   From luxury's contagion, weak and vile!
> Then, howe'er crowns and coronets be rent,
>   A virtuous populace may rise the while,
> And stand a wall of fire around our much-loved Isle."

GENERAL INDEX.

A

	PAGE
Absenteeism,	149
Ainslie, Mr, of Costerton,	89
Ainslie, J. A.,	58
Andersons of Whitburgh,	70, 129
Anderson, Major-General,	21, 129
Anderson, Rev. W.,	134
Armet Water,	4, 70
Augustine, Order of St,	41

B

Beacons on Soutra Hill,	54
Beatsman's Acres,	51
Bell, The,	76
Blackshiels,	23
Blackshiels Inn,	18
Blythe, Rev. James,	124
Borthwick, William,	62
Boundary Commissioners,	19
Brotherstones,	69, —
Brothershiels Burn,	4, 70
Brothershiels,	14
Broun, Mr,	71

C

Cairns, Dominus Thomas,	83
Cakemuir Burn,	3
Cakemuir Castle,	17
Candelabra of Church,	75
Carkettill, Rev. Patrick,	85
Carlyle, Rev. Dr.,	90
Carmichael, Rev. P.,	85
Cavers, Rev. Walter,	87

	PAGE
Character of the People,	143
Charities,	121
Charlie, Prince,	20
Charlie, Prince—Relics,	21
Chesterhill,	72
Churchyard,	77
Communion Cups,	75
Cooper, Rev. John,	126
Creichton, David,	10
Crombie, Mr,	67

D

Deanburn,	3
Deil's Putting Stone,	61
Divisions of Soutra Parish,	53
Dixon, Thomas Griffies,	66
Dun, Mr,	69

E

Edinburgh Lord Provost, &c.,	50
Edmonstouns of Fala,	8
Eldon, Lord Chancellor,	26, 129
Extracts from Kirk-Session Records,	111, 115

F

Fala Dam,	19
Fala, Derivation of Word,	1
Fala Flow,	16
Fala Hall,	22
Fala House,	12
Fala Kirk,	6, 73

General Index.

	PAGE
Fala Luggie,	16
Fala Moor,	5, 15
Fala Rectory,	7
Fala Smith,	28
Fala Village,	23
Falconers,	64
Farm Works,	147
Fawlay, Agnes de,	8
Feu-duties,	68
Fletcher, Robert,	63
Food of the People,	146
Frank, Rev. W.,	84
Fraser, Rev. W.,	127
Friar's Well,	44
Frostineb,	18

	PAGE
Gala Water,	3
Gilston,	67
Girthgate, or Sanctuary Road,	5
Gourlay, Rev. J.,	91
Grant, Rev. A.,	87

H

Hamilton, Patrick,	11
Hamilton, Thomas,	11
Hamilton M'Gill, Thomas,	12
Harkness, Rev. W.,	95
Hastie, Rev. James,	84
Hay, Sir Edmund,	7
Hay, Sir William,	8
Henderson, Rev. James,	84
Home Life,	146
Horn, Mr,	67
Humbie,	71
Humbie Woods,	1
Hunters' Hall,	57

I

Inglis, Lord-Justice General,	67, 128
Ingram, Rev. James,	97

	PAGE
Inquisitiveness,	144
Invasion of Hertford,	55
James V.,	14, 23
James VI.,	24
Johnston, Rev. George,	87
Johnston, Sir William,	125
Johnstounburn,	63, 70
Johnstoune, Rev. A.,	84

K

Keith-Marischal,	71
Keith, Rev. Jas.	124
Kellybaak,	70
King's Inch,	30, 57
King's Road,	54

Land Question,	149
Lawrie's Den,	57
Libraries,	121
Linndean,	4, 66
Logan, John, Poet,	130
Logan, Rev. J.,	86
Lords Excommunicated,	25
Lothian, M. J.,	67

M

Maitlands,	64
Maitland, D., of Soutra,	113
Malcolm, King,	31
Manners of the People,	145
Manse, The,	78
Marriages, Irregular,	115
Mary of Gueldres,	45
Mary's, Queen, Charter,	50
Masters of the Monastery,	42
Meusdenhead,	63

General Index.

	PAGE
Mill of Monastery,	44
Ministers,	84
Monastery, Wealth of,	31
Monteith, Rev. Mr,	89
Mort Cloth,	77
Munro, Rev. T.,	96

N

Nairne of Dunsinnane,	74
Napier, Lieut.-Col.,	65, 129

O

Ogilvie, Mrs,	65
Ogilvie, Thomas E.,	65

P

Paraphrases, Scottish,	123
Parochial Board,	117
Patronage,	79
Pogbie,	64
Political Excitement,	139
Politeness,	145
Pope Gregory's Charter,	38
Population,	138
Porteous, Rev. James,	85
Prebendaries of Trinity College, Edinburgh,	47
Presentation, Sale of Right of,	81
Pringles of Soutra,	51
Prior's Well,	44
Provost of Trinity College, Edinburgh,	47

Q

Queen, Jubilee of the,	55

R

	PAGE
Reading of the People,	144
Records of Kirk-Session,	110
Reidhall,	64
Religion of the People,	143
Rental,	137
Roads of the Parish,	5
Ruins of Monastery,	40
Rural Character of People,	141

Sand-glass,	75
Schools of Fala,	117
Schoolmasters of Fala,	120
Secession Church,	123
Sherriff, Rev. Thomas,	94
Shootings,	137
Sinclair, Sir William,	8
Singers, Rev. Archibald,	91
Simpson, Rev. Patrick,	88
Skirving, Adam,	89
Soutra Charters,	31
Soutra, Derivation of Word,	1
Soutra Monastery,	30
Soutra Sanctuary,	40
Soutra, Situation of,	1
Soutra Vicarage,	50
Soutra Village,	57
Sprott, Rev. William,	91
Stipend of Fala,	100
Stipend, Valuation of,	102
Sunday Observance,	148
Surety Men,	56

T

Tenants of Farms,	135, 136
Thomson, Rev. J. F.,	98
Thomsone, Rev. Thomas,	85
Tokens for Kirk,	76
Transfer of Revenues, &c.,	45
Trinity Well,	39

General Index.

	PAGE
Trinity College, Edinburgh,	45
Tyne Water,	3

U

United Presbyterian Church,	123

V

Valuation of Stipend,	102
Vicars of Soutra, R.C.,	49

W

	PAGE
Wages,	137
Walter of Moravia,	37
Watling Street,	5, 30, 54
Wealth of Monastery,	37
Wight, Mr,	17
Witch of Soutra,	58
Whitburgh,	50
Wood, Lord,	66, 129
Wood, J. A.,	67
Wotherspoon, Rev. W.,	91